Thriving Amidst the Chaos: Finding Hope in Revelation

Roger VanderKolk & Jeff Chitwood

Blauw Shack Media

Blauw Shack Media

ISBN: 979-8-9867313-2-2 (paperback)

Cover Art by Kirstin Vincent

I would like to dedicate the book to Bob Lowrey, a distinguished Professor at Lincoln Christian College and Seminary. Bob taught me and inspired me to study the book of Revelation and to always be a student of the Word. - Jeff Chitwood

I would like to dedicate the book to Edna Townsend, my maternal grandmother. Grandma Edna always had faith that I would someday be a writer, long before I had even considered it. Thank you for believing in me. - Roger VanderKolk

Table of Contents

Foreword

This book is our message to you, the reader. Thus, it is written mostly in a first person format. For the most part, we will speak together. But for those occasions where differentiation between authors is noted, we will call out the specific author in the headings.

The book of Revelation is arguably the most studied and written about book in the Bible. As such, most of the background material in this book is considered common knowledge because it is available from multiple sources. If there is a construct or idea that is tied only to a specific author, we provide credit in the Bibliography / Notes section.

We wrote the book to inject a message of hope into our world today. A person only has to watch the first few minutes of a news broadcast on any network to be reminded that our world is a mess.

PART ONE

PREFACE

Introduction

Does the world *really* need another book about Revelation? We are confident that you have not read a book that interweaves the strengths and capabilities of a pastor skilled in expository preaching with a layperson that dissects spiritual truths for application to daily living. Between us, we have studied the book of Revelation for decades to understand the message for today's generation (Ok, so in clear transparency, the pastor is responsible for 95%+ of that study and analysis). Do you need another book on Revelation? Consider this instead: Would a book that gleans spiritual truths for today's culture from the book of Revelation help your daily life?

The title of the book was specifically chosen to answer the question of how we can thrive in spite of the state of our world today. We are living in a time of constant upheaval and feel that the term "chaos" is appropriate to describe our culture. Webster defines the word "chaos" as: "a state of utter confusion; a confused mass or mixture; the inherent unpredictability in the behavior of a complex natural system".

Webster defines the word "thrive" as: "To grow or develop successfully; to flourish or succeed; to progress toward or realize a goal despite or because of circumstances". It would seem therefore, that the word "thrive" is almost an antonym of the word "chaos". Is it possible to glean information from the book of Revelation, a book that was written nearly 2,000 years ago, that would help us in our world today? The answer is Yes!

The purpose of this book is to share strategies for living in hope despite today's chaotic environment. Sound good? Read on.

Who is Jeff Chitwood?

Who am I? Basically a sinner saved by grace! God has blessed me more than I deserve and I owe Him more than I can ever hope to repay. Let me quickly share my story with you.

As a teenager I became involved in the youth group at church and eventually gave my life to Christ. Throughout my high school years there was a tug of war going on when it came to deciding what I wanted to be when I grew up! God won the tug of war and I entered Lincoln Christian College in Lincoln, IL. I was a ministry major and graduated Cum Laude with a Bachelor of Arts Degree. I then entered Lincoln Christian Seminary majoring in New Testament Theology. I tell people that I squeezed a three year degree into seven years! While in college and seminary I served as Youth Minister at South Shores Christian Church in Decatur, IL, on a part-time, then full time basis (1978-1982). I completed my seminary degree while serving full time as Youth Minister at South Side Christian Church in Springfield, IL (1982 - 1995). During my undergraduate and graduate degree programs I always strove to incorporate what I learned in the classroom into the real life experience of ministry in the church.

After serving in the Youth Ministry for seventeen years I transitioned to the Senior Ministry. I continued to serve at South Side Christian Church as the Sr. Minister for the next fifteen years. When I turned fifty I had a ministry colleague and former college professor ask me a haunting question, "Jeff, what are you going to do with the second half of your ministry life?" That led me into searching what God had in store for me and it led me to a small church in Southwest Florida called Anchor Christian Church. At Anchor I found a congregation full of mature people but who were still eager to serve and learn the Word of God. I began serving at Anchor in 2010 and at the time of this writing, 2024, am still serving there as Sr. Minister.

I always strive in my teaching and preaching to correctly present the truth of God's Word and apply it to life today. Simply understanding the background and history of the Bible is not enough. God's Word is living and "sharper than a two-edged sword". It is my goal to always be cut to the heart by the Word of God and to share His Word with others.

All of the above I owe to the grace of God. He has blessed my journey with a wonderful wife, Judy, and two daughters, Crista and Heather.

Who is Roger VanderKolk?

If you've read any of my previous books, you know that I am just a guy sitting at his computer, hoping that the words being typed not only make sense, but that they bring hope to the reader. I feel blessed and humbled that God opened doors that enabled me to be in this position.

After a fairly normal childhood and adolescence, I chose to continue my education at Indiana Wesleyan University, a small Christian liberal arts college in Indiana. It was there that I felt God calling me to the ministry. The calling was so strong that after a year of pursuit of other majors, I switched to Christian Ministries. My goal was to be a Youth Minister. The remainder of my schooling was focused on learning the tools of ministry: the thorough examination of the text of the Bible, expository sermon preparation, counseling, and many other pursuits to be able to effectively pastor a church.

But life doesn't always work out how we want it to work out. After graduation, I was unable to secure a ministry position and was forced to work in the business world to pay the bills. The word "business" is perhaps a little strong: I went back to the world of retail, working the same job that I had during high school. The job was ok, but it wasn't challenging, and if we are being honest, it didn't pay all the bills. So I began to seek employment elsewhere.

I had an acquaintance at church who had a sales and marketing job at a local manufacturer. I really had no idea what he or the company did, but I started pestering him about whether a job was open at his company. One day he said yes. I interviewed, was hired, and thus embarked upon a 25+ year career in sales and marketing roles at various companies. I was blessed throughout my career: I was able to travel the world; I formed relationships with colleagues around the globe; earned my MBA; and experienced the joy of having customers' lives improved from products I helped bring to market.

In 2018, my father passed away unexpectedly. Dad and Mom had recently moved to Florida, many hours from my home in Minnesota and my brother's home in northern Illinois. As the eldest son, we decided that I would move to be closer to Mom. In 2019, I moved to southwestern Florida. I was fortunate to work remotely for my employer at the time in the same community as Jeff Chitwood and his family lived. Jeff had been a part of our family's life when he ministered in Springfield and this helped to ease my transition from the land of 10,000 frozen lakes to an area defined by sand and sunshine.

In another of life's re-directions, I found myself with more spare time so I resurrected a previous dream of writing. During his fight with various types of cancer, my Dad had kept a journal designed to provide hope to others in similar struggles. Using his journal as the foundation, I began writing a series of books designed to provide hope to people fighting serious diseases. If you find yourself in a similar struggle, I encourage you to look into these books. The series is called "Thriving Amidst Adversity" (additional details and ordering information can be found at www.blauwshackmedia.com).

"Thriving Amidst the Chaos" is the first book in a new series. This series is intended to continue on the theme of bringing messages of hope into the world, albeit to a different audience. These books are intended to help *anyone* that finds life difficult. In other words, everyone. My prayer is that it brings hope into your journey as you navigate in the world today.

One final tidbit: my maternal grandmother was a life-long educator who wrote a series of books designed to help young children learn to read. She always believed in my early attempts at writing and encouraged me to be an author. I'd like to think that she is looking down from heaven, happy that I am finally pursuing her dream for me. Thank you, Grandma Edna!

Partnership (Roger)

It's somewhat amazing that Jeff agreed to participate in this project considering he has known me for nearly 40 years. I can still remember when Jeff (and his wife, Judy) accepted the position of youth ministry at our church in Springfield, IL. Despite all of the typical teenage behavior I exhibited (or perhaps, because of that behavior), Jeff and Judy quickly became a guiding influence in my life. Time spent at youth group, ministry projects, and Bible Bowl trips strengthened this relationship. When I came home after college one spring and indicated that my degree required a youth ministry internship, Jeff was gracious enough to bring me on board at church. I learned a lot in that position: how to work with youth, the correct way to build programs, how to influence people, and many more life skills.

I say all of that to say this: throughout all the years spent with Jeff, the depth of his knowledge of the book of Revelation is without equal. Jeff has the perfect amount of scriptural knowledge which, combined with his grasp of the Greek language, results in thoughtful analysis of a complex book of the Bible.

As our society continues to trend towards chaos, I feel compelled to look to the Bible for answers on how to live. Specifically, how we can lean on the hope found in the book of Revelation. There is no better person that I could partner with to bring this message to people.

How to Approach the Bible

There are many ways to approach the Bible. It can be approached as a book to be studied from a historical perspective, endeavoring to find and verify the facts that are given. It can be approached from a scholarly perspective that seeks to dissect it and analyze it. It can be approached from a spiritual perspective, seeking to discern God's Word in your life. Which is the best way to approach it? All of the above.

We may never be able to grasp all that there is to learn in the Bible, but that does not mean that we should not study it and let it speak to us. Let this study of the book of Revelation be one that challenges us in all areas of our life, mind, and soul.

We believe that the Bible is the inspired word of God as spoken to believers throughout history. These words were recorded in written form by people of faith and passed down for generations. Although there are numerous accounts of this period of time recorded throughout history, those found in today's Bible passed rigorous qualifications before they were added to the Bible.

If your beliefs do not line up with the above, we ask you to approach this book with an open mind. The book of Revelation speaks to everyone.

What the Book Is / Isn't

Chaos isn't new to modern times. The world has been in a state of chaos since the beginning of human civilization. However, throughout history, one book has stood the test of time. The Bible was relevant hundreds of years ago and it is still relevant today. There are many messages of advice, instruction, and hope that have inspired people throughout the centuries. We believe this also includes the book of Revelation.

Therefore this book isn't intended to be put onto a bookshelf somewhere to gather dust. The intention is to read it. Then read it again at a later date. Go beyond simply reading the book and use the study guide to make it relevant for your life.

Dig Deeper with Study Guides

The book of Revelation is complex; the exact meaning of the various elements and symbolism have perplexed theologians throughout the centuries. We do not expect this book to resolve any of those long-standing mysteries but instead offer this book as a practical guide to applying the book of Revelation to our daily lives.

We encourage you to do some additional research and learn more about the book of Revelation. Therefore, at the conclusion of each chapter, there is a section of questions designed to further stimulate your quest for knowledge. The best practice for this section is to get involved with friends, neighbors, or family members to start a study group. Collective knowledge is usually stronger than the thoughts and opinions of an individual, and learning should increase as a result.

At minimum though, we encourage you to study and reflect on those questions. This exercise will not be wasted as you look at the book of Revelation for messages of hope for today.

The First in a Series

This first book will spend a lot of time on the background of the book of Revelation. It is important to understand the author, the historical setting of the book, the culture of the world at the time, and the persecution of the early church. We then build upon that foundation to focus on Revelation, chapter 1, which is the Introduction to the book. From there, we focus on the letters to the seven churches of Asia, which are the second and third chapters of Revelation. Three chapters may not seem sufficient for a standalone book, but there is a tremendous amount of content contained the following pages. We actually found ourselves trimming content to keep the book size manageable.

The remainder of the series will be as follows:

- Book 2: The throne room in Heaven and the opening of the seven seals. (chapters 4-11)
- Book 3: The seven trumpets, the woman and the dragon, and the seven bowls of wrath (chapters 12-17).
- Book 4: The fall of Babylon, Christ's Return, and the new Heaven and the new Earth (chapters 18-22).

We are excited that you have picked up this book and started reading it. While this book has substantial messages of hope, many more messages of hope will be found within the entire series and we encourage you to continue reading beyond this first book.

One More Thing

With the exception of direct quotes from the Bible, we will never recognize the devil as a proper noun in any of our writings. He doesn't deserve the recognition that comes from being a proper noun. We realize that we may be alone in this thinking, but this is the hill we choose to defend. As we're responsible for entering the text into the book format, this is how he will be designated in this book "satan".

PART TWO

HOW THEN TO THRIVE?

Faith: The Foundation to the Path Forward

The concept of thriving amidst chaos is borrowed from the series of books that dealt with Bruce VanderKolk, Roger's father, and his battle with multiple types of cancer. But this is OK, because Roger is the author of that series and doesn't mind if they are plagiarized by this book.

As you will read throughout the remainder of this book, we believe it is easier to embrace a thriving mentality within a relationship with God. Nothing brings hope more than the knowledge that, despite all of the conditions of our environment and the world, our troubles are only temporary. Something far greater awaits those who have Hope in God.

Bruce found a way to thrive in the midst of the chaos of his battle with life-threatening cancer. The following is an essay that he wrote stating his faith as the foundation of being able to thrive despite serious health challenges. Although the essay was written during his battle with bladder cancer, the message applies to his earlier diseases as well. We feel it is important to set an understanding with readers that our foundation for thriving in the chaos of our world is built upon Bruce's words.

"He will not fail us" (Bruce VanderKolk)

Psalm 91 (NIV)
1 "Whoever dwells in the shelter of the Most High
 will rest in the shadow of the Almighty.
2 I will say of the Lord, 'He is my refuge and my fortress,
 my God, in whom I trust.'
3 Surely he will save you
 from the fowler's snare
 and from the deadly pestilence.
4 He will cover you with his feathers,
 and under his wings you will find refuge;
 his faithfulness will be your shield and rampart.
5 You will not fear the terror of night,
 nor the arrow that flies by day,

6 nor the pestilence that stalks in the darkness,
  nor the plague that destroys at midday.
7 A thousand may fall at your side,
  ten thousand at your right hand,
  but it will not come near you.
8 You will only observe with your eyes
  and see the punishment of the wicked.
9 If you say, 'The Lord is my refuge,'
  and you make the Most High your dwelling,
10 no harm will overtake you,
  no disaster will come near your tent.
11 For he will command his angels concerning you
  to guard you in all your ways;
12 they will lift you up in their hands,
  so that you will not strike your foot against a stone.
13 You will tread on the lion and the cobra;
  you will trample the great lion and the serpent.
14 'Because he loves me,' says the Lord, 'I will rescue him;
  I will protect him, for he acknowledges my name.
15 He will call on me, and I will answer him;
  I will be with him in trouble,
  I will deliver him and honor him.
16 With long life I will satisfy him
  and show him my salvation.'"

I am always amazed when those who have cancer outwardly appear to have a tranquil nature. I wish I could copy that DNA of tranquility into my own mind and personality. Maybe they are at peace with their situation and the outward appearance is real and not a brave front. Unfortunately, my situation has been displayed as that of a chameleon. To others I change my color to reflect an appearance of strength and acceptance. I try not to take the cancer seriously in front of others and when asked I reply, "I'm doing ok". I live a life externally of pretending that nothing really is wrong and a philosophy of "this too will pass-no big deal".

But it is a big deal; I just do not want to admit it outwardly. Besides, I have found that many people who have not experienced the trials of cancer do not want to talk about it, do not understand the emotions a person goes through, may even avoid you as if you have leprosy. My situation may even remind them of their own personal experience of cancer or of someone who had cancer and they do not want to bring to surface from the depths of their mind the pain that they have gone through. This is where my other chameleon color comes in.

When alone my mind is in turmoil; it is constantly making my daily life one of contrasts, like a yo-yo that is ever moving up and down. One moment I may be up and the next I may be at the bottom of the yo-yo's cycle; a cycle that is in perpetual motion denying the laws of physics. I am in a 24/7 mode of operation as there appears no escape from the reality of cancer. It is there with you when you wake up, it is there with you in the morning hours, it is there with you when you go to the store, it is there with you when you may be entertaining, it is there with you when you're watching television at night, it is there with you when you go to bed and you pray to God for healing, it is there when for some reason you wake up during the night; it is always present, never ending. How do you explain that to someone who has not walked in the same shoes and does not have a grasp of the terrible experiences that cancer brings? In some ways, I think the mental aspects of dealing with cancer may be as bad or worse then the physical aspects of dealing with cancer.

I wish I had a magic formula to give you as you go through many trials, but I do not. Well intended people may say "just rely upon God", "out of adversity there comes good", "I know you will be ok", or "there are a lot of new treatments today that will help you". Well, thanks but this does not help. Sure, I appreciate their sincerity and attempts at giving hope, but words alone do not provide peace of mind; words do not heal.

I may sound cynical and maybe I am to some extent. However, as I have tried to come to grips with my cancer, I know I could not continue without drawing upon the strength given to us through our belief in God and the many comforting verses found in His Word. Does it totally solve my daily mental gyrations? No, but I cannot imagine what it would be like without His love and care for me to minimize those gyrations. I wonder how do those with cancer who do not have a relationship with God ever make it through the day? Where is their hope? The answer is they have no hope! You see I believe God truly understands my situation. And I fully understand that my way may not be His way.

There are many great Bible verses that give comfort and strength. Some of my favorites are found in the book of Philippians, such as:

"Rejoice in the Lord always. I will say it again: Rejoice! Let your gentleness be evident to all. The Lord is near. Do not be anxious about anything, but in everything, by prayer and petition, with thanks-giving, present your requests to God. And the peace of God, which transcends all understanding, will guard your hearts and your minds in Christ Jesus. Finally, brothers, whatever is true, whatever is noble, whatever is right, whatever is pure, whatever is lovely, whatever is admirable-if anything is excellent or praiseworthy-think about such things. Whatever you have learned or received or heard from me, or seen in me-put it into practice. And the God of peace will be with you." Philippians 4:4-9 (NIV).

And:

"Forgetting what is behind and straining toward what is ahead, I press on toward the goal to win the prize for which God has called me heavenward in Christ Jesus." Philippians 3:13b-14 (NIV).

Finally, I return to the scripture quoted at the beginning of this writing, Psalm 91 (NIV): A Psalm of hope and comfort. How can we not find solace when we read the following about God?

- We will rest in the shadow of the Almighty
- He is my refuge and my fortress, … in whom I trust
- He will save you
- He will cover you with his feathers
- Under His wings you will find refuge
- His faithfulness will be your shield and rampart
- He will command his angels concerning you to guard you in all your ways
- He will protect you, when we acknowledge His name.

- He will be with you in trouble
- He will deliver you and honor you

Do I expect my life to be a "bed of roses" because I put my trust in His words of hope and comfort? No. Do I expect that this life will pass away and there will be a more glorious life for eternity with our Lord and Savior? Yes.

May you seek comfort in knowing that what is coming is far greater than what you are going through now.

Bruce W. VanderKolk (5 November 2017)

Life is Hard

One of the most over-used phrases is that "Life is Hard". It generally is followed by a second phrase such as "get up" or "suck it up" that is meant to encourage the listener to overcome the hardness of life.

The reality is that yes, Life is Hard. Period. End of Story. A bit of faith coming in, but if you are a believer, the Bible makes it plain as day that life isn't a bed of roses. Sin has entered our world and we will never experience a life that is truly easy. Sure, we will all experience times of peace, but during those times, the universe is in the background planning, plotting, and scheming on how to bring pain, loss, or something equally as devastating back into our lives.

Psychology tells us that there are five stages of grief: Denial, Anger, Bargaining, Depression, and Acceptance. The process is the same for everyone faced with devastating, life-changing circumstances, ultimately leading to the final stage of acceptance. Work continues after acceptance; we must still determine how to move forward with life.

When faced with circumstances and fear that can easily overwhelm us, three options are available:

1. We can surrender. We can give up and let the chaos win. We can withdraw from society, friends, family and wait for chaos to burn the world.

2. We can survive. We can only do what is necessary to come out on the other side of our circumstances. We can throw all of the strength and resources that we can pull together to beat the chaos.

3. We can thrive. Building upon the choice to survive, we can fight the chaos. We can also work to ensure that our lives enrich those around us, whether it be family, friends, acquaintances, or society as a whole.

In the face of worries that choke the positivity out of our lives, we will face the choice of one of these three options. However, life isn't fair: once we make a decision to choose one option such as to thrive, life will continue to tempt us to change our minds. Even those who decide to thrive will face the temptation of surrendering.

What it Means to Thrive

Whenever we are faced with a difficult situation, the immediate focus is just to survive the episode so that we can live to fight another day. There is absolutely nothing wrong with pursuing the survival path because it is valid: As finite creatures, we need to make sure that we do everything in our power to extend our life on this earth.

The problem comes when the survival path is the only path we choose. When the focus is solely on survival, after we are successful there is no further action moving forward. This is limiting not only for the person going through the battle but for society as a whole.

As Bruce fought through his battles with cancer and other diseases, he came to realize that there are two types of thriving:

1. Thriving Internally - The first stage of thriving is learning how to flourish in spite of difficult circumstances. How to wake up in the morning and get out of bed. How to get the head and emotions in a good spot.

2. Thriving Externally - The second stage is taking the internal flourishing and applying it to help others. Thriving is the act of blessing the lives of others. It is focusing not on your difficult situation, but on how to improve the lives of others.

As you begin the "meat" of this book, we encourage you to take notes and thoughtfully consider how to embrace the concepts gleaned from Revelation so that you can thrive today, tomorrow, and for the rest of your days.

If you read any of the Thriving Amidst Adversity books, you are familiar with the format of interspersing keys to thriving amidst Bruce's journal. We will follow this structure with this book as well: look for sections titled "Roger's Ramblings" and "Points to Ponder with Jeff".

Revelation's Theme and Thriving

The theme of Revelation can be summed up in two words: "We Win". Those who have accepted Jesus are those defined as "we" while the word "win" describes the victory of Christ that enables His followers (Christians) to have victory over the power of death. The book of Revelation offered messages of hope for the first century believer and it still offers hope for us today.

We hope these are helpful as you navigate today's world.

Part Three

Revelation's Relevance

Relevance to the Audience

Imagine for a moment that you are a first century Christian living in the bustling city of Ephesus. You are married, have a few kids, and work hard to provide for your family. Your father was a fisherman, his father was a fisherman, and his father was a fisherman. Needless to say, the apple doesn't fall far from the tree and you also are a fisherman. It's a hard job: You wake up before dawn to get the boat prepared and onto the water. You then spend all day casting nets into the water to catch enough fish to feed you, your crew, and perhaps even to sell in the market for others in the city. Unfortunately, the modern fishing rod hasn't been invented so you and your crew use every muscle in your body to throw gigantic nets over the side of the boat. And that's the easy part. When you pull them back up into the boat, the amount of fish in the nets is such that the net can sometimes be so heavy that you can't get it back into the boat. After working on the water all day, eventually you make it back home after dark to hopefully catch some sleep before waking up to repeat the cycle tomorrow. The difficulty level of the job is greatly increased when the area you fish is beset by stormy weather. Many days after a storm, you feel lucky enough to actually make it home at night.

A few years ago, you were invited to the home of a friend on the Sabbath Day (no work on the Sabbath). You are surprised when you arrive to see that there are several other people at your friend's house. After the meal, they start worshiping a God that you are unfamiliar with, but the message of the worship and teaching intrigues you. As you leave your friend's house, you promise to come back, bringing your wife and children as well. After several visits, your family has decided that they want to experience the same level of joy that the other people have and you make the decision to follow Christ and become Christians.

Life is great. Yes, the work is still hard, but now you have a purpose: To serve God with everything you do, including your work. Your crew has noticed a difference and many have become Christians themselves. Life certainly is great.

Until it isn't. Because you start hearing alarming news about fellow Christians being persecuted simply because of their beliefs. The persecution is awful, and sometimes hard to imagine what people would do to their fellow human beings. You hear of Christians being fodder for the Colosseum and other venues. You hear of apostles being beheaded or crucified upside down for preaching about Christianity. You hear of Christians being burned alive and used as lamp posts in Rome. Simply horrific. You start to worry about whether you, your family, and your church are safe or if persecution will become rampant in Ephesus.

This sounds like a frightening scenario, right? But that is exactly the condition that Christians were experiencing during the time that John was recording his vision while he was on the island of Patmos. Was the letter relevant? Were the messages of holding fast, standing firm, and persevering relevant? Was the message that "We Win" relevant? Absolutely!

Relevance to Christians Throughout History

When John recorded on paper the visions that he experienced, he was writing to the seven physical churches that were in existence in Asia at that time. As we will continue to learn, each of these churches was faced with a particular set of circumstances that required improvement in order to accomplish their mission of bringing people into Christianity. John offered encouragement to the churches as well because times were challenging for the new believers.

But in reality, John's letters were written to the children of the believers and their grandchildren and their great grandchildren. The messages of the letters were relevant to believers in the Dark Ages, the Enlightenment, the 1700's, the 1800's, and Christians in the twenty-first century.

Take for example the recent period of time defined as the "Cold War" when the dominant fear of the world was nuclear war. Do you think the messages of the book of Revelation was relevant for society during that time? You betcha.

The book of Revelation needs to be studied as if it is timeless. Which of course it is. Consider for a moment the sheer numbers of people that have been affected by John's letters. Let's assume that every twenty years marks the start of a new generation (this might be aggressive, but older birth rates during our time are likely offset by historically younger birth rates). This means that for every one hundred years, there are 5 generations of people. Since the year 90 AD, there have thus been 19 periods of one hundred years. After adding the generation immediately after John, there have been approximately 96 generations of people since John wrote his letter.

The message of Revelation was relevant to John's audience but also to the 96 generations of human beings since the letters were written. The messages of holding fast, standing firm, persevering, and that "We Win" have been sources of encouragement for millions of believers.

Relevance to Believers Today

Our world is increasingly becoming post-Christian. Headlines proclaim that church attendance is at all-time lows and is trending downward. People are being sued (i.e., persecuted) for acting consistent with their religious beliefs. Society is giddy when laws are passed that seemingly contradict Biblical principles. on-line social "warriors" enthusiastically seek to ruin the lives and livelihoods of those they disagree with on cultural issues.

Is the book of Revelation relevant to Christians today? Yes! This is foundational for this book and future books. As you study Revelation you will find hope, encouragement, and keys to living in our society.

Relevance to Our Society

Allow us to stand on our soap box for a brief moment of time. We believe that society is generally a better place when everyone practices the "Golden Rule": "So in everything, do to others what you would have them do to you, for this sums up the Law and the Prophets." (Matthew 7:12, NIV).

Modern society has hijacked several mutually beneficial concepts under the guise of progressivism. The danger to society as a whole is if you do not participate in "culture think", you are to be exiled from society. Take for example the concept of tolerance. The previous definition, based on biblical principles of liberty and freedom, is that we need to be tolerant of each other. This is out of respect because we are "fearfully and wonderfully made" (Psalm 139:14, NIV). We are all the same: mostly good but have some areas where we need to improve. Regardless of our differences, we are to love each other.

As the world becomes increasingly post-Christian (i.e., more non-Christians than Christians), this new ideology has come to embrace the concept that tolerance only exists when we all believe the same. If someone believes differently, they are "in-tolerant" and must repent or risk being ostracized from society. This type of culture will turn on those whose ideologies don't line up 100% with the media, the "flavor of the day", and those on social media. Even if they are not a believer in Christ, sooner or later, the politically correct machine will come for them.

If you are one of those who are not following Christ, consider the message of Revelation again and you will note that it is relevant to you during our times. Hold Fast. Stand Firm. Persevere. These are all important parts of the book of Revelation. But even more important is the message that "We Win". As we begin to study the keys to thriving in today's climate as found in the book of Revelation, we ask you to keep an open mind so that you might eventually be "written in the Lamb's book of life." (Revelation 21:27, NIV)

PART FOUR

THRIVING IN CHAOS (REVELATION CHAPTERS 1-3)

Deep Dive into Revelation

Why Study the Book of Revelation?

Why in the world would anyone want to study Revelation? Everybody seems to have their own reason. Some say, "I want to find out what the end times are going to be like." Some say, "I want to try and figure out what all the beasts and bizarre scenes mean." Others say, "I don't want to study it at all because it just scares me and doesn't make sense."

Well, let us give you a good reason for studying the book, in fact it is the best reason but we never hear anybody giving this reason. Listen to these amazing words:

"The revelation of Jesus Christ, which God gave him to show his servants what must soon take place. He made it known by sending his angel to his servant John, who testifies to everything he saw — that is, the word of God and the testimony of Jesus Christ. Blessed is the one who reads the words of this prophecy, and blessed are those who hear it and take to heart what is written in it, because the time is near." (Rev 1:1-3, NIV)

The best reason for studying Revelation is to be blessed by God. That blessing will come if we listen to His message and obey what it says. The last phrase also reminds us of a very important point – the time is near.

What does that mean? This life as we know it is not all there is. There will come a day when Jesus will return and God will usher in eternity. When will that happen? We don't know. But ever since Jesus ascended into heaven after His resurrection, we have been living in the last days. John tells the Christians in the first century, and he tells us today, to be ready and be faithful, because each day brings us closer to the return of Jesus.

Helpful Reading

As you read the book of Revelation, you will be well-served to read other books of the Bible as well. These books provide background information and some amount of context to John's writings.

We recommend reading the following books of the Bible:

- Genesis - You have to read, at minimum, the story of Creation and the subsequent fall of man.
- Isaiah - There are many prophecies found in this book of the coming of Jesus to the world.
- Gospels - There are four: Matthew, Mark, Luke, and John. These should all be read as they have a unique approach in explaining Jesus's time on the Earth.
- Acts - An account of the formation of Christianity.

Or, you could just read the entire Bible. We acknowledge that this sounds daunting, but many reading plans are available on-line that will allow you to read the entire Bible over the course of a year. Just something to consider.

What to Avoid when Studying

Before we share our thoughts about what specifically you should study in the book of Revelation, we are going to share some of the pitfalls and traps that we have experienced so that you may avoid them. In other words, let us help you avoid our mistakes.

First, be careful about attaching a great amount of significance to specific details. For example: the identity of the Anti-Christ. Too often throughout history, there have been countless attempts at labeling a specific person as the Anti-Christ. During the 1940's, many people no doubt labeled Hitler as the Anti-Christ. But we are still here, the battle of Armageddon didn't occur, so Hitler was not *the* Anti-Christ (He may have been *an* anti-Christ, but more on that later). When you read the book and want greater clarification (such as the identification of the Woman and the Beast), take a step back and read the text to understand the greater concepts that are being communicated. As we will discuss in the next section, the literary tool of "symbolism" comes to play as we study Revelation.

Our second piece of advice is to remember that the book of Revelation was written to the early Christian church. But as it was divinely inspired, it has relevance to Christians throughout the course of time. We may be thinking that the "Doomsday Clock" is nearly midnight, but if you were to ask people during the 1800's, they probably would have said the same thing.

With that being said, our third piece of advice is that even though we may or may not be living in the final end times, the Bible is quite clear that we are to live as if we are in the end times.

Finally, our last piece of advice is to not use this book as your only study guide. We are not Biblical scholars. We are just a couple of guys who want to bring hope and encouragement into the world from selected tidbits from Revelation. If you would like to study in greater detail, then we encourage you to go on-line or to purchase material that is specifically designed for in-depth study of the book of Revelation.

Guidelines for your Study

First and foremost, pray, asking God to give you understanding.

Second, when you read through the book of Revelation, look for the "Big Picture" message rather than trying to visualize all the images. What is happening? Is God receiving glory? Are believers being attacked? The message for us might be to give God glory during rough times.

Third, remember that there are different ideas and different ways of interpreting Revelation. If someone's interpretation is different than yours, don't make it a test of faith. Agree to disagree. Be Respectful.

Finally, write down questions and don't be afraid to ask those questions to others. Perhaps you can start a discussion or study group of Revelation. We have always found that the more voices and opinions present in a group, the greater the understanding that is applied to the study.

Symbolic Language Defined

A simple definition of symbolism would be anything which suggests or stands for a meaning in addition to its ordinary meaning. It is a sign which suggests a meaning rather than stating it. It is a representation in fact or vision of one thing or event which has no meaning or significance in itself but only in what it portrays.

Why use Symbols or Symbolic Language? When you were younger did you ever write a message in a secret code or use "invisible ink"? Why did you do it? What are some possible reasons why Jesus would have used symbolic language? He may have wanted to communicate a message to the Christian who would understand the symbols but at the same time keep the meaning from non-Christians who had no knowledge of what those symbols meant.

General Characteristics of Symbolic Language in the Bible

Symbolic language in Revelation is meant to present a message of hope and judgment. It portrays the concept of dualism – the conflict between good and evil. It is used to express concern for the end times. It also contains visions, angels, dreams; these are used to communicate a message of the spiritual dynamic involved in the work of God.

Understanding the historical and cultural background is important in helping to find meaning in symbolic language. Many times the symbols reflect what is going on in periods of persecution. In Revelation there are references to the martyrs that have suffered. This is a picture of what was going on in the first century as well as throughout history since then.

Symbolic language contains an element of prediction. It is prophetic because it brings a person to the judgment of God. Other places in the Bible where symbolic language can be found are: Isaiah 24-27 and 56-66; Zachariah 9-14; Joel 2,3; Ezekiel; Daniel 7-12. In these Old Testament passages a message is given to the people of the prophet's day but also a message that is projected to the future generations. This approach is also found in Revelation.

Guidelines in Interpreting Symbolism

Symbolism may give heightened dramatic effect, not necessarily having an independent meaning in every detail. The symbols are to be interpreted, rather than visualized. Look at the following example that someone has given of what the Old Testament book of Song of Solomon would "look like" if taken literally.

"How beautiful you are, my darling!
    Oh, how beautiful!
    Your eyes behind your veil are doves.
    Your hair is like a flock of goats
    descending from Mount Gilead.
    Your teeth are like a flock of sheep just shorn,
    coming up from the washing.
    Each has its twin;
    not one of them is alone.
    Your lips are like a scarlet ribbon;
    your mouth is lovely.
    Your temples behind your veil
    are like the halves of a pomegranate.
    Your neck is like the tower of David,
    built with elegance;
    on it hang a thousand shields,
    all of them shields of warriors."
    (Song of Solomon 4:1-4, NIV)

Obviously, the Song of Solomon is presenting more than just a literal picture. If you literally visualize a woman who looked like that, it would not be an appealing picture. Solomon is communicating the aspects of beauty of a woman by using language that symbolically represents beauty and value. Those images, in the proper context and culture, present a powerful image of a woman any man would be honored to have as a companion. So, beware of forcing symbols to fit into your own schemes. Seek to understand the cultural setting in which symbols originally appeared. One must not begin to press details of symbolic language. Details belong to the overall picture. Recognize man's finite capacity to understand the infinite things of God. John was trying to describe a heavenly vision and heavenly creatures with earthly words.

Symbolic Language and the Book of Revelation

"The locusts looked like horses prepared for the battle. On their heads they wore something like crowns of gold, and their faces resembled human faces. Their hair was like women's hair, and their teeth were like lion's teeth. They had breastplates like breastplates of iron, and the sound of their wings was like the thundering of many horses and chariots rushing into battle". (Revelation 9:7-9, NIV)

And we say John wanted to present a message! Then what in the world is he talking about in the passage above? Why does it seem so confusing to us today? In Revelation John used special language and writing styles to communicate his message. To understand it we need to have a grasp of symbolic language in the Bible.

Before we dismiss Revelation for being totally unreal we need to realize that we use symbols and "word symbols" everyday of our lives. There are many different types of beasts in Revelation but what about the animals we use today to symbolize things: America, the eagle; Russia, the bear; China, the dragon; Democrats, the donkey; Republicans, the elephant. These facts should lead us into realizing that we need to study some principles of interpretation if we are to understand the symbols in Revelation.

Work through the simple exercise below and see how you do at interpreting some of the symbolic language in Revelation. Read the passage listed. First, see if the symbol is interpreted for you, if not, then try to interpret it by the language and images used. Second, see if you can see the message that the scripture might give us today.

- Revelation 1:12-20 - Picture of Christ in Power
- Revelation 5:1-10 – Portrait of Christ, especially from Old Testament imagery
- Revelation 14:6-13 – Worship of the beast – This section of scripture is greatly enlightened by the following cultural and historical information. During the time of John writing Revelation, the Christians would have been very familiar with "worship of the beast". The Roman emperor Domitian (Roman 81-96 AD) took the title "lord and god" and ordered people to confess he was "lord and god" as a test of loyalty.

How prevalent was the imperial cult in Asia Minor? Of the seven cities mentioned in Revelation 2-3, five had imperial priests and altars (all but Philadelphia and Laodica) and six had imperial temples (all but Thyatira). At Pergamum an imperial temple was established as early as 28 B.C. The city was so central to the imperial cult that Revelation describes this city as having the "throne of satan." In short, a Christian in Asia Minor could not avoid the Imperial Cult.

Some Symbols in Revelation and What They Mean
- 7 Lampstands = The 7 churches.
- One standing among the lampstands = Christ.
- Lamb = Christ.
- One sitting on the throne = God or Christ.
- Rider on the White Horse in Chapter 19 = Christ.
- Beast = Satan or objects of idol worship.
- Great Prostitute = satan.
- 7 Seals = Communicating a message of trial and persecution.
- 7 Trumpets = Communicating a message of warning of coming judgment.
- 7 Bowls = The wrath of God on the evil.
- Number 7 = Denotes completeness, occurs 54 times in Revelation.

Symbols where used in the first century and still are used today to communicate a message. Here are some examples:

- Symbol of the Fish was used to designate that someone was a Christian. Why? If each letter of the Greek word for fish is used as an acronym, they stand for the following:
  - Iota (i) is the first letter of Iēsous (Ἰησοῦς), Greek for "Jesus".
  - Chi (ch) is the first letter of Christos (Χριστός), Greek for "anointed."
  - Theta (th) is the first letter of Theou (Θεοῦ), Greek for "God's", the genitive case of Θεός, Theos," Greek for "God."

- ◦ Upsilon (y) is the first letter of (h)yios[7] (Υἱός), Greek for "Son".
  - ◦ Sigma (s) is the first letter of sōtēr (Σωτήρ), Greek for "Savior."
  - ◦ Put together, they communicate the message of "Jesus Christ, God's Son, Savior).
- Symbol for Christ that consisted of two Greek letters.
- Dove representing peace.
- Anchor representing hope and security.

As you continue throughout this book series, remember the importance of a high level understanding of symbolism.

Introduction to the Book of Revelation

The easiest way to introduce Revelation is to present and lay out a foundation of the "big picture" stuff. There are different ways to approach a study of Revelation. As we mentioned at the beginning of the book, Jeff has spent much time studying Revelation. His approach has been influenced by his education. Normally he wouldn't share this but it is relevant to his approach. He graduated from Lincoln Christian Seminary with a Master of Divinity Degree in New Testament Theology and one of his major professors was a leading expert on Revelation. The professor, Dr. Bob Lowrey, published one book and unfortunately passed away after a battle with cancer before he could write additional books. Jeff wrote a couple of papers on Revelation while taking several classes under Dr. Lowrey.

Having said all of that, let us assure you that we will not answer all the questions that you have about Revelation. In fact, we will probably raise a few more you have never considered. But in the end we want to claim the promise of Revelation 1:3 that God will bless us for hearing His words to us and taking them to heart. The big picture message, no matter the details or approach of your interpretation – God is in control and His plan will be carried out. One day this earth will pass away and He will usher in eternity.

So, let's begin this journey together with the prayer on our hearts that God will teach us what we need to know so that we will be ready when that day comes. Our study of the book of Revelation has revealed a few truths about the book, which we will share below.

Truth #1: Revelation was not written to confuse people.

But it is confusing to us because in the pages of Revelation you will find bizarre images and strange creatures. There is a beast with 10 horns and bronze claws, stars falling from the heavens, and a great red dragon with 7 heads. There's the mark of the beast – 666. There are bowls of sulfur, bowls of wrath, and a bottomless pit. There are the four horsemen of the apocalypse. It is full of strange stuff and images that are foreign to us.

One of two things usually happen when people read Revelation – they run away from it or they fixate on the details of it. They run because it scares them – it is easier just not to think about it or deal with it. Fixation can lead to trying to interpret details to the "nth" degree and try to place a spiritual meaning to everything. There are passages in Revelation that interpret themselves but the interpretation only gives the meaning of the big picture, not all the details of the scene. Or, some only look for something that relates to the latest thing in their culture or the latest headline.

We need to understand that John was using images that the people in those days would have understood much better than us. Hopefully as we go through this study of Revelation we can understand some of these images more easily. John uses language and symbols to communicate a message just like we do today, without even realizing it. John's style is different than the gospels or one of the letters. It is called Apocalyptic Literature – meaning it is prophecy, which many times uses images and visions to communicate its message. In the Old Testament this writing is found in the books of Ezekiel and Daniel.

But what seems strange to us may not have been all that strange to the people of the day. The language and images used may have been common to them. Without thinking about it, we do the same thing in our culture. Is it unusual for you to think of America when you see a picture of a bald eagle or the red, white, and blue of the American flag? That imagery is very familiar to us. Do you think of good and beautiful things when you see a picture of a serpent surrounded by darkness and red glowing eyes? You probably think of evil.

Our challenge then is to seek to understand the images that John is using in the context of the time and culture from which they came. We need to take a historical and contextual approach to Revelation. Meaning, as we go through Revelation we want you to look at the context in which it was written and see some of the imagery and history of the time when it was written. By doing that we can get a better understanding of the message that God wants to communicate to His people throughout the ages.

Truth #2: Revelation was written with a purpose

Some people think the book was written just to tell us when Jesus will come back. The topic is addressed but that is not the driving message of the book of Revelation. The purpose was to encourage and give hope to Christians who were going through uncertain times and exhorting the believers to remain faithful in their faith until the day Jesus returns.

Does it give us times and dates for the end times? No, but neither did Jesus. The teaching of Jesus in the Gospels, as well as His words in Revelation, teach us that we need to live our lives every day like it could be our last. He wants us to be found walking and living out our Christian faith, even when it gets tough.

Truth #3: Revelation was written to real people in real churches who were facing real problems.

We will look at those people and churches in Revelation chapters two and three. These will be some of the easiest chapters to go through. From a historical context, the people John was writing to were facing persecution from an evil Roman ruler. It was written during the Rule of Domitian, 81-96 AD. He brought about the second major persecution of Christians. The first was from Nero in 64 AD. What he did and who he proclaimed to be played a major role in Revelation's depiction of the beast that wanted to be worshiped. He was hated by even the Romans. After his death the Roman Senate passed a decree that his inscriptions should everywhere be erased, and all record of him obliterated.

It was during this time that God led John to write the book of Revelation to answer the question on the hearts of the Christians: "Is there any hope?" It was written to encourage the believers to hang in there – to give them hope. It is believed that some of the images and language John used would have been understood by the Christians but not necessarily the Romans who opposed them. This may have been important in a world that opposed Christianity to the point of putting Christians to death. John used the phrase "lamb that was slain" for example. Who do we know that refers to? Jesus. But to a Roman official it wouldn't have communicated that.

Truth #4: Revelation is written to help us see Jesus better

In order to understand this truth, you need to ask yourself the following question: "How do I see Jesus?" Most modern day pictures and movies portray a kind, gentle Jesus: long flowing robe, long brown hair, kind, polite, and proper. In some ways we get an image of a meek and mild Jesus, almost a Mr. Rogers-like Jesus who went around teaching people to be nice to each other.

We remember growing up knowing what a tough guy looked like. In movies there was John Wayne. Rough and rugged and always came out on top. In cartoons there was Popeye the Sailor Man. Crazy big arms and when he ate his spinach he could beat up anyone! There were guys like Chuck Norris as Walker Texas Ranger, Sylvester Stallone as Rocky and Rambo, Arnold Schwarzenegger as the Terminator, and Clint Eastwood as Dirty Harry – "Go ahead. Make my day."

So, if someone was to come along and ask us to name the top five most fearsome guys we could think of, we probably would not have mentioned Jesus. We don't think we are alone in that. Not too many other Christians would either. But Jesus is more imposing than we sometimes think. Especially in the book of Revelation.

Don't get us wrong, we are not saying Jesus should be thought of as some divine "Dirty Harry". But too often the church suffers from a condition that someone dubbed J.D.D. – Jesus Deficit Disorder. It's not that we don't think about Jesus; it's that we don't think big enough about Jesus. It's like we're seeing him through the wrong end of the telescope – He looks smaller and farther away than He really is. Our fear is that too many of us have settled for a meek and mild Jesus rather than the "King of Kings and Lord of Lords".

Truth #5. Revelation presents a powerful picture of Jesus

After some words of introduction and an explanation that he is exiled on the island of Patmos for preaching the gospel, John then begins to write down what was happening to him:

"I, John, your brother and companion in the suffering and kingdom and patient endurance that are ours in Jesus, was on the island of Patmos because of the word of God and the testimony of Jesus. It was the Lord's Day, and I was worshiping in the Spirit. Suddenly, I heard behind me a loud voice like a trumpet blast. It said, 'Write in a book everything you see, and send it to the seven churches in the cities of Ephesus, Smyrna, Pergamum, Thyatira, Sardis, Philadelphia, and Laodicea.' When I turned to see who was speaking to me, I saw seven gold lampstands. And standing in the middle of the lampstands was someone like the Son of Man. He was wearing a long robe with a gold sash across his chest. His head and his hair were white like wool, as white as snow. And his eyes were like flames of fire. His feet were like polished bronze refined in a furnace, and his voice thundered like mighty ocean waves. He held seven stars in his right hand, and a sharp two-edged sword came from his mouth. And his face was like the sun in all its brilliance." (Rev 1:9-16, NIV)

That doesn't describe a meek and mild Jesus. It depicts a powerful Jesus. He is standing among the lampstands – which John interprets for us and tells us that those were the churches. Jesus wasn't floating around on a cloud playing a harp, He was in the midst of His people. He was dressed in a robe with a gold sash – clothing of a king. His head was white like wool – not a mark of frailty or aging, but a symbol of his deity and dignity. His eyes were "like blazing fire" piercing through the layers of stuff we try to hide behind. His feet were like polished bronze, representing strength and stability. His voice thundered like mighty ocean waves – a voice of power and majesty. A sharp two-edged sword came out of His mouth. When He spoke, it was with authority and finality. Finally, His face was like the sun in its brilliance – the glory of God poured out of Him. Does that describe a weak Mr. Rogers-like Jesus to you?

The text is not confusing: Jesus is Lord. The point is clear: be warned! Jesus is not a kindly grandfather who tussles our hair when we misbehave and says, "Well, boys will be boys." Jesus is not a smiling buddy who winks at our sin and lets us do what we want. He is a towering and powerful figure who will not be managed. He is Lord. He is in the midst of His church. He knows our shortcomings. He knows our needs. He knows our sins, and He is big enough to do something about them.

The real question we need to ask of this passage is not, "I wonder what the third star in His right hand stands for?" The question we need to ask is, "How do I see Jesus?" When we are in the presence of someone we deem important, we get a little nervous. Our hearts beat faster, our palms sweat, our tongue gets tied, and we might not be sure of what to do.

Consider another question: "When you walk into the sanctuary on a Sunday morning, does your pulse quicken? Do you catch your breath? Do your palms get sweaty? Do you get a little nervous? You should, because when you enter into worship you are in the presence of the King of Kings and the Lord of Lords.

Did you catch what John's reaction was to all of this? He was scared to death. In Revelation 1:17, John writes, "When I saw him, I fell at his feet as if I were dead." How did Jesus react? "That's right, you vermin, you worthless being, bow to me!" No, this is what He did: "But he laid his right hand on me and said, 'Don't be afraid! I am the First and the Last. I am the living one. I died, but look—I am alive forever and ever! And I hold the keys of death and the grave.'" (Revelation 1:17-18, NIV) How reassuring! This great big Jesus is imposing, but He is also comforting. As He stands among His church – as imperfect as it is – He says, "I've got you"

Here is the conclusion as you start this journey. Actually, maybe that's the word you need to hear today. "Conclusion". If you are afraid, if you are facing some things you don't know how to handle, if you are struggling with a sin that is keeping you from being all you can be in Christ - here is the good news: It is not a meek and mild Jesus looking out for you. It is the King of Kings and the Lord of Lords and one day He is coming back for you.

With Him – We Win!

Chapter 1 (The Introduction)

Overview

Are you ready to dive into Revelation? If so, then chapter one is a great starting point because it is referred to as, surprise, surprise, the "Introduction". There are twenty verses, which is about the normal length of a chapter in the book of Revelation. What is interesting however, is that John abandons his standard practice of starting his letter with a greeting to the reader and body of believers. Instead, he uses the first three verses to convey the legitimacy of the content of the letter to his audience. Once he has assured his audience that the letter is God's message, rather than his own, John greets the audience.

One of the more challenging books of the Bible to understand, the first chapters of Revelation are easily understood because they contain encouragement for the early church. But from there, the book dives into prophetic visions of the end times. There are likely as many interpretations of the visions as there are people that have read the book of Revelation. And the truth is, this side of heaven, we won't be able to grasp it all because our mental capacity to comprehend all the prophetic messages is limited.

John describes the reason for his stay on Patmos and the manner in which he received the visions that would form the foundation of the letter to the early churches. Intermixed amongst this greeting are passages of worship and depictions of the glory of Jesus when John received the vision.

World Conditions when Revelation was Written

It is impossible to ignore the role of Christianity in history. The impact that this new religion had on the Roman Empire is documented in so many different historical records, that its existence is undeniable. The Roman Empire, arguably the greatest empire in the history of mankind, was affected and altered by Christianity.

It is necessary for us to understand the events that were occurring in that ancient world. Later we will use this foundation to draw comparisons between the time of John and our world today.

Geopolitical Climate

From an objective standpoint, the world has always been in a state of chaos: people often choosing to fight rather than to try to solve their disagreements through discussion and diplomacy. Families have fought families. Cities versus cities. And of course, countries have constantly been at war with each other. The history of every region of the world is marked by conflict. Chaos has reigned supreme.

Maybe the saddest form of chaos has been when the strong or those in authority exert dominance and persecution over the weak or defenseless as happened in the days of John's writing. Take, for example, the area we refer to as the Middle East. Arguably, the Middle East has seen more than its share of strife and chaos, having seen numerous conflicts. From the Babylonians to the Assyrians to the Greeks to the Romans to the Crusades; even to this very day, this area has rarely been without chaos.

Persecution

One of the most significant political issues of the first century was the political deification of emperors. Many of the Roman leaders and emperors thought of themselves as gods, beginning with Alexander the Great and various Roman emperors. Julius Caesar was praised as a god manifest and the savior of the whole human race.

The first two centuries A.D. had three emperors in Rome who proclaimed themselves divine: Gaius (37 - 41), Nero (54 - 68), and Domitian (81 - 96). Gaius had his sister deified and he eventually came to believe in his own deity. He required worship from those in his court and even had a temple erected to himself in Rome. Nero had his image put on coins declaring himself god. When Rome burned in 64 AD he needed a scapegoat and blamed the Christians. He did many detestable acts, including covering the persecuted Christians with tar and putting them on a post and lighting them as human torches in his gardens. Domitian was declared "Master and god" as early as 89 AD and oaths of loyalty were required by his subjects. Those who rejected the worship of emperors were suspected of being a traitor.

Persecution of Christians continued after Domitian into the next century with the Roman emperor Trajan. Emperor worship brought political and religious issues to the forefront. The Christians had to decide if they wanted to be loyal to the emperor or loyal to God. In the first century it was more than a choice of preference, it was a choice of life or death. For example, a Roman governor by the name of Pliny sent a letter to the Emperor Trajan around 112 AD, sharing with the emperor how he was handling Christians through various types of persecution to the point of death.

Thus, the theme of remaining faithful and holding on until the end can be found woven throughout the pages of Revelation:

- Revelation 2:10 – "Be faithful, even to the point of death, and I will give you the crown of life." (NIV)
- Revelation 14:12 – "This calls for patient endurance on the part of the saints who obey God's commandments and remain faithful to Jesus." (NIV)
- Revelation 17:14 – "They will make war against the Lamb, but the Lamb will overcome them because he is Lord of lords and King of kings — and with him will be his called, chosen and faithful followers." (NIV)

Early Church

The cradle of Christianity is found in the area today known as Israel. Israel was restored as a nation following World War II. The area had formerly been known as Palestine. This 7400 sq mile piece of ground on the eastern shore of the Mediterranean Sea (a little smaller than the state of New Jersey) has seen more turmoil than almost anywhere else in the world. Since the day God told Abraham to go to the land which He would show him (Genesis 12), that area of the world has seen numerous changes of ownership.

Jesus was born into a land full of God's chosen people, the Jews, yet they did not rule the land. In 63 BC Rome conquered the area and began to rule over the land of Palestine. Jesus and Christianity started in a region that had a built-in conflict with Rome. Rome allowed local governments a certain amount of self-rule as long as they pledged allegiance to Rome and paid their taxes promptly. Many of the governors were considered "puppet" rulers who were in place to enforce the over-arching laws of Rome. The Jews resented Rome's rule and taxes but they appealed to it's authority in getting rid of Jesus. Soon after Jesus's death, burial, and resurrection, His followers, later known as Christians, began to function as the church in Jerusalem.

The history of the church's spread from Jerusalem throughout the Roman dominated world can be traced in the books of the gospels and the book of Acts in the New Testament. The following are passages that mention believers being sent "out into the world" to spread the good news of Jesus and His message of salvation:

- Mark 6:7-13 - Jesus sent out the twelve apostles to pave the way for his ministry, paying particular attention to calling for people to repent.
- Luke 10: 1-24 - Jesus sent out 72 followers to towns and places where he was planning to visit. One of the most infamous verses for mission work is found in this passage: "The harvest is plentiful, but the workers are few. Ask the Lord of the harvest, therefore, to send out workers into his harvest field." (Luke 10:2, NIV)
- Acts 2:42-47 - The early Christians were devoted to each other and spread the message of salvation amongst their friends, neighbors, acquaintances, and communities. As a result, "the Lord added to their number daily those who were being saved." (Acts 2:47, NIV)
- Acts 4:36-37 - At some point, Christianity made it to the island of Cyprus because in this passage we find a descriptor of an early believer, Joseph, who was described as a "Levite from Cyprus" (Acts 4:36, NIV).
- Acts 8:1-8 - After the persecution and killing of Stephen, the Bible makes reference to the fact that "all except the apostles were scattered throughout Judea and Samaria" (verse 1, NIV) and "Those who had been scattered preached the word wherever they went". (verse 4, NIV).

There are many more records of early believers spreading the message of Christ throughout the book of Acts. Research and read about Philip, Barnabas, Peter, and Paul.

Diaspora

The Bible tells us that the entirety of Jesus's ministry was focused in the lands of Israel and modern-day Palestine. With Jerusalem and Nazareth as the nexus points, the geographical coverage of the ministry was roughly 100 miles long by 30 miles wide. To put it another way, the area of ministry was roughly twice the size of the state of Rhode Island. The churches to which John wrote the book of Revelation were over 1,000 miles by land from Jerusalem. In an age without modern modes of transportation, how exactly did Christianity spread to an area that was more than a 45 day walk away?

Ironically, Roman domination of the Mediterranean world actually helped the spread and growth of Christianity. The Pax Romana was a period of peace – the "peace of Rome". Four things enabled the spread of Christianity during this time. First, there was peace across the empire and people could travel from country to country without fear. Second, travel was made easier by a road system throughout the empire, enhancing trade, the sharing of ideas, and allowing people like the Apostle Paul to easily go from one town to another. Third, the Greek culture and language became universal, thus communication and the sharing of ideas became easier. Finally, Rome had a tolerance for different religions, unless they were seen as a threat to Rome.

Rome would tolerate Christianity up to a point but its tolerance had reached its breaking point by the time John wrote Revelation. It was too late, however, because like an epidemic, Christianity had already spread throughout the Roman Empire. This was due in no small part to the persecution because when large groups of people are persecuted, they tend to move and migrate to areas with less, or even no, persecution.

This theory proved accurate throughout the early formation of Christianity after the death of Jesus. Followers who were persecuted in their homeland would migrate to new geographies where they would eventually convert people to Christianity. Those in power would notice and, fearing a loss of power, would start persecuting Christians, which then led to more Christians moving away from the persecution to new areas. This cycle repeated itself throughout the Roman Empire for generations.

Those in power had not yet realized the universal truth that the fastest way to spread an idea is to attempt to squash it. By the time that John was exiled onto Patmos, Christianity had spread well beyond the Holy Land.

The Church circa 90 AD

Church history tells us that there were approximately 55 years between the start of Christianity and when John received his vision and wrote the book of Revelation. That is a lot of time for any new religion to spread throughout the known world.

Christianity did, in fact, expand during this period of history, quite extensively. Believers spread Christ's message throughout Asia Minor (modern day Turkey), the Aegean Peninsula (Greece, Macedonia), all the islands in the Mediterranean, and even to Sicily and Italy. We are not going to embarrass ourselves by guessing the number of Christians at that time, but it was substantial.

At this point in time, it should have been clear to all concerned, including the Romans, that Christianity was not going to become extinct. The number of believers continued to increase.

But so did the persecution from the Romans and the other religious leaders of the day. It was to this persecuted group of Christians that John's letter was written, with the express intent of offering encouragement to the believers. Encouragement that they win in the end.

Chain of Custody

"The revelation from Jesus Christ, which God gave him to show his servants what must soon take place. He made it known by sending his angel to his servant John, who testifies to everything he saw — that is, the word of God and the testimony of Jesus Christ." (Revelation 1:1, NIV)

From the very first words at the beginning of the first chapter of the book of Revelation, John makes it clear that he is not messing around. His opening remarks are strong indicators that this letter is different from his other letters and writings. The implication is that the audience needs to pay immediate attention to the letter and read it as soon as possible. John's first words are: "The revelation from Jesus Christ, which God gave him to show his servants what must soon take place." (Revelation 1:1, NIV). Notice that John doesn't open this letter with greetings, salutations, or even a mention of his role in the church. No, he gets right to the important stuff and basically informs the audience that he is simply the last person in the communication chain for this message.

Did you ever play the game "Telephone" in school or at church youth group? The concept is simple: line the kids up and whisper a secret to the first person who then whispers it to the next person and so on until it reaches the last child. What was the message that the last person in line received? Most likely, it was different from the message whispered to the first person. Why? Because we are horrible communicators and struggle to consistently deliver to others the same message that we received.

We assume John recognized this fact about the human condition and it is one of the reasons why he abandoned his usual greeting in favor of a message that immediately spoke to the legitimacy of his message. It's almost as if he was telling his audience that they need to pay attention because the letter is directly from God.

Read the verse again. Notice that John says the message came from God, was delivered to Jesus, who communicated it to John, who was writing the message to the early believers. Talk about a game of telephone where you do NOT want to misinterpret the message!

Another word for John's approach is found in law enforcement circles and is called the "Chain of Custody". The US National Institute of Standards and Technology (NIST) defines this concept as the "process that tracks the movement of evidence through its collection, safeguarding, and analysis life-cycle by documenting each person who handled the evidence, the date/time it was collected or transferred, and the purpose for the transfer". The purpose of a strong Chain of Custody is to safeguard the evidence. If there is a problem with the Chain of Custody of drugs seized from suspects, there is a huge risk that the evidence will be ruled as illegitimate and not considered in the suspect's trial. If the chain of custody is tainted, the evidence is worthless and thrown out. This is so important that virtually every law enforcement organization has professionals that are solely tasked with ensuring a strong Chain of Custody.

John felt it necessary to establish a strong "Chain of Custody" at the start of the book of Revelation. This message was of such importance that he was not going to take any chances for his readers to consider it as faulty. Much like a prosecutor will not take anything for chance during an important criminal trial, John wasn't going to take any chances either. By establishing the strong Chain of Custody ("The message directly came from God through Jesus to me"), he was telling the early believers to pay attention to the rest of the letter.

Roger's Ramblings: Truth Today

"Who testifies to everything he saw-that is, the word of God and the testimony of Jesus Christ" (Revelation 1:2, NIV).

Continuing on with the courtroom analogy. We've all seen courtroom scenes in the movies and on television where the witness is called to the examination stand and is told (not asked) to swear that their testimony is the truth, the whole truth, and nothing but the truth. The implication in our judicial system is that if the witness deviates from the truth there are consequence, most notably a potential prison term for lying under oath. The judicial system considers this such an important aspect of the trial that a name has been given to the action of lying under oath: perjury. The consequences of perjuring oneself are severe; do so at your own risk.

As we start to discover the significance of the book of Revelation in our daily lives, it is important to understand the significance of the above verse. Other versions of the Bible translate the second verse of the first chapter of Revelation as follows:

- *"Who bare record of the word of God, and of the testimony of Jesus Christ, and of all things that he saw." (King James Version)*
- *"Who has testified to and vouched for all that he saw [in his visions], the Word of God and the testimony of Jesus Christ." (Amplified Bible)*
- *"Who bore witness to the word of God, and to the testimony of Jesus Christ, to all things that he saw." (New King James Version)*
- *"Who bore witness to the word of God and to the testimony of Jesus Christ, even to all that he saw." (New American Standard Version)*

What is interesting is the commonality amongst the versions of the Bible regarding the usage of the word "testimony". This shouldn't come as a big surprise because as we learned previously in this book, it was important to John to tie his writings to a firm foundation. The particular word that John uses in the original Greek language is "marturia" which is translated as evidence, usually given in a judicial setting. What's even more interesting is that John uses this same word 13 times throughout his writings that are included in the New Testament. It is clear that John wanted to establish that his writings were every bit as truthful as what is used in our judicial system of today.

But why is this important to us today, living in the 21st century? We believe that the word "truth" has lost it's meaning to our society. Throughout history, the battle between right and wrong has always been based upon some level or authority or truth. Most often, these concepts were based upon the Bible, but in some cultures they were based upon other religious documents and creeds, leaders, science, etc. But presently in our society, truth as an absolute concept has nearly disappeared. It is vital to discuss this situation as you begin reading since it is not to be taken lightly. We often now observe in our culture little evidence that society will move back to absolute truth. (This is likely also the reason why John uses the first paragraphs of his letter to the new believers to convey the importance of absolute truth as well.)

Take a minute and ask yourself: "What does our society consider truth?" If we take an objective look at society, and are honest with ourselves, our society believes in multiple truths rather than the absolute Truth. For example: The ease of access to a large audience on social media has lowered the barrier to entry of news organizations. Suddenly, everyone can be a "journalist" and present "truth" to their followers and audience. More times than not though, this truth isn't truth at all; it is simply an excuse to skip fact-finding and present things that support an individual's narrative. Our society has created a culture where truth can be different for everyone. "My truth" has replaced "The Truth".

This culture shift is dangerous. What happens if my truth and your truth collide? How do we know who is in the right and who is in the wrong? If someone's truth is that they are entitled to possess expensive watches and other jewelry on display in a store, at what point will conflict arise when the store owner's truth says differently? Sure, the law of the land supports the owner's truth, but laws can be changed. Consider the following passage from 2 Peter:

"But there were also false prophets among the people, just as there will be false teachers among you. They will secretly introduce destructive heresies, even *denying the sovereign Lord who bought them—bringing swift destruction on themselves. Many will follow their depraved conduct and will bring the way of truth into disrepute. In their greed these teachers will exploit you with fabricated stories. Their condemnation has long been hanging over them, and their destruction has not been sleeping." (2 Peter 2:1-3, NIV)*

Is it any wonder then, why the word "truth" can be found 40+ times in the writings of John in the Bible? Interestingly enough, the word itself is not used in the book of Revelation, but that is certainly due to the fact that John establishes its veracity through his "chain of custody" passage.

As you move forward with this book, your study in Revelation, and your quest to thrive in our world, consider from what source you derive truth.

How Soon is Soon?
"...what must soon take place." (Revelation 1:1, NIV)

When someone says to you, "I will get back with you soon", what goes through your mind? Is "soon" a short time or a long time? If you and the person who said it have a totally different concept of "soon" it could lead to surprise if "soon" happens quickly or frustration if "soon" takes it time. "Soon" is one of those words that implies a period of time but no specific amount of time is assigned to it.

John uses the word "soon" three times (Rev 1:1; 11:14; 22:6) to refer to the things that were going to take place as he is writing down what he is being shown about God's plans for heaven and earth. Jesus uses the word "soon" five times (Rev 2:16; 3:11; 22:7; 22:12; 22:20) in the context of urgency, calling His followers to heed His words. All of the uses point to something in the future that will take place.

So, how "soon" is "soon"? In the context of Revelation, only God knows but the word is used with a purpose. The word is used to depict something that will surely happen, but the exact time that it will happen is intentionally left vague. Why? Because every generation of the followers of Jesus need to live with the tension of the "already and not yet". On this earth we have "already" experienced many of the blessings of God but we have "not yet" fully received nor comprehended the vastness of God's blessings.

Jesus wants us to face the chaos of this life with the certainty of His promises. In the book of Revelation there is a lot of chaos presented but at the end of each section of chaos there is a period of worship and peace. It is that peace that the word "soon" promises. "Soon" implies to hang in there and be patient because the current state you find yourself in is not permanent. Our challenge is to not impose our idea of "soon" onto God's plan. On a temporal timeline we measure everything by the calendar and the clock whereas God measures time in light of eternity. Jesus speaks His final words in Revelation in the context of eternity – "Yes, I am coming soon" - and John replies with a temporal time line prayer – "Amen, come Lord Jesus!" The implication is that John is saying, "Hurry up, make 'soon' happen quickly." But God doesn't work with the temporal, He specializes in the eternal. It is in the eternal that we will truly enjoy the blessings of an existence without "chaos."

Blessed Readers

"Blessed is the one who reads aloud the words of this prophecy, and blessed are those who hear it and take to heart what is written in it." (Revelation 1:3, NIV)

Would it surprise you to learn that the first word in the verse above, one of the first verses in the book of Revelation, is used in many other places in the Bible? As a matter of fact, the word "blessed" is found over 200 times in the New International Version (NIV) translation. Clearly this is an important concept that the nearly 40 writers of the Bible wanted to communicate to their audience: "Pay attention to these words and your life will be blessed". But what sort of blessing exactly did they have in mind?

Thankfully, we have the original Greek language to fall back on as it provides a greater appreciation for John's message in verse 3. The Greek word used in verse 3 is "Makarios" and is translated as being supremely blest and by extension fortunate and well-off. Well now, that increases our clarity as to what was on John's mind when he was writing the letter. John didn't just want his readers to be happy, but to be supremely blessed by what they were going to read in his letter. It should come as no surprise then that John uses this exact word six other times in the book of Revelation. (Coincidentally, this is the same word that Jesus uses in the Sermon on the Mount as found in the fifth chapter of Matthew)

Let's re-phrase verse 3 therefore with what we have learned:

"Supremely blest is the one who reads aloud the words of this prophecy, and supremely blest are those who hear it and take to heart what is written in it." (Revelation 1:3, our translation)

One more point of discussion before we dive even deeper into Chapter 1. Go back and read those translations of verse three. Notice anything consistent between the translations? In order to receive the benefits of the letter, John encouraged his readers to embrace three actions: First, READ the letter. Secondly, HEAR (or listen) to the words, emphasizing the importance of paying attention and not letting their minds wander. Finally, John tells his audience to DIGEST the messages. He wanted the believers in the seven churches in Asia to take to heart the messages and apply them to their lives. The book of Revelation was meant to be an agent of change, modifying the behaviors and actions of the early believers.

We believe that this message remains valid today. Read. Hear. Digest.

The Blessing Paradox

In *"Thriving Amidst Cancer II: A General's Focus on Hope While Fighting Bladder Cancer"*, Roger encouraged readers to increase the positivity in their lives by realizing how they are blessed on a daily basis. Whenever we feel negativity increasing it's hold on our lives, we need to realize that we woke up today and are thus blessed. We are blessed when we are able to eat and sleep indoors. We are blessed when we have love and support from family and friends. We are blessed that a loving God made the decision to bless our lives.

So what do the verses of Revelation 3 and Matthew 5 have in common? They tie in the blessed outcome to behavior. In other words, being blessed, being "supremely blest" requires action on our part. Consider the following verses from the fifth chapter of Matthew's gospel where he states that "blessed is/are":

- "The poor in spirit" (verse 3, NIV)
- "Those who mourn" (verse 4, NIV)
- "The meek" (verse 5, NIV)
- "Those who hunger and thirst for righteousness" (verse 6, NIV)
- "The merciful" (verse 7, NIV)
- "The pure in heart" (verse 8, NIV)
- "The peacemakers" (verse 9, NIV)
- "Those who are persecuted because of righteousness" (verse 10, NIV)
- "You when people insult you, persecute you and falsely say all kinds of evil against you because of me." (verse 11, NIV)

Did you notice the common theme with the beatitudes listed above? They are all internal qualities that are manifested externally. The passages above are pulled from Jesus's Sermon on the Mount, which was delivered early in His ministry. This speaks to the importance of the message: it is our calling to be a blessing to others. In order to participate in God's supreme blessing, we must be humble, comfort those who are mourning, show mercy, make peace with others, suffer for Jesus's name, etc.

How much could our society improve if more people decided to be a blessing to others? If we didn't engage with those on-line social "warriors" with whom we disagreed? If we treated the coffee shop barista with humbleness rather than treating her like a second-class citizen? If we sat down in the break-room at work and chatted with a co-worker dealing with loss?

Let's approach today thanking God for his blessings to us, but let's also be a blessing to those around us. Focusing on ourselves and not those around us is easy because our core nature is one of selfishness. Focusing on others will not be easy. But there is a shortage of people living externally in our society. Focusing on others, despite how are are feeling, being a blessing to them, that's how we thrive amidst the chaos of today.

The Author

"John, To the seven churches in the province of Asia." (Revelation 1:4, NIV)

We do not need to spend much time on who wrote the book of Revelation because it is revealed in the opening verses of Revelation: "The Revelation from Jesus Christ, which God gave him to show his servants what must soon take place. He made it know by sending his angel to his servant John, who testifies to everything the he saw-that is, the word of God and the testimony of Jesus Christ." (Revelation 1:1-2, NIV)

The message of Revelation comes from Jesus Christ, revealed by an angel to John, who wrote it down. This is a very clear statement about the authenticity and authority of the book of Revelation. Authenticity and authority are important when revealing what God has in store for the future.

God chose John to write down this very important message. This John is the apostle John that we find in the Gospels. He is also author of the Gospel of John and the three epistles of 1 John, 2 John, and 3 John. He had a real relationship with Jesus as an apostle and God chose him to record the very important message we find in Revelation. John spent the bulk of his life spreading the good news of Jesus. He was, in one word, devoted. (For a more detailed and insightful look at John as a person/author, see Part 7 in the back of this book.)

Roger's Ramblings: Devotion

"And immediately they left the boat and their father and followed him." (Matthew 4:22, NIV)

"He was, in one word, devoted"

History tells us that neither John nor James left Jesus's ministry and returned to fishing. Not only did they "immediately" leave their old lives behind them, but they stayed the course with their new lives. Were there bad days, days when they probably looked back with longing on their time fishing? Probably. Sure, fishing was hard and being on a boat on seas notorious for bad weather wasn't safe, but they weren't under constant threat of death by the Romans. Yet, despite all of the persecution and danger, they stayed with Jesus.

Why did they stay? Because they were devoted to the cause of hope for our world, ardently dedicated and loyal to Jesus's message. And the hope that Jesus offered to the world is the same hope that John offers his readers in the book of Revelation.

To understand the implications of devotion for John and James, a deeper inspection is required. Did you realize the following about John and James?

- *They were with Jesus during his entire ministry, roughly 3 years. John and James were so devoted to Jesus that they spent over 1,000 days with him.*
- *They left family behind. For a culture where the lifestyle was family-based, that would have been extremely difficult for all the family. There would have been no family feasts when times were good and no collaborative mourning when times were bad.*
- *John and James left a lucrative business behind when they followed Jesus. When John and James walked away from the fishing boat, they walked away from their father's business. Zebedee would have needed to replace two hard workers that were likely in their prime physical working years, probably a tough task. And there is the matter of inheritance of the family business. Perhaps there were other sons besides John and James, but if not, Zebedee would not have been able to hand the business down to his offspring.*
- *They traveled with Jesus all throughout the land of Palestine during the ministry when travel was much rougher than it is for us in the twenty-first century. Jesus and the disciples most likely walked from town to town, over sandy, rocky ground in elemental sandals. Travel by ship was risky due to the storms on the water. Yet, despite these hardships, John and James endured because they were devoted to Jesus and his ministry.*
- *After Jesus returned to Heaven, John and James continued with their ministry in the time of Roman persecution with the constant threat of imprisonment, beatings, and even death.*

By now you may be asking, "How does being devoted translate into thriving in chaos?" The answer is that when we are devoted to something outside of ourselves it provides a focus to our lives and turns the chaos of the outside world into minor challenges, rather than major obstacles. That is assuming that we are devoted to the right things. But how do we define what is right in our lives?

Every one of us is devoted to at least one thing, if not dozens. An example of devotion in our society is our devotion to those small electronic devices that we hold in our hands and carry with us everywhere. We are so devoted to these devices that we get anxious when we are separated from them, if even for a few minutes. Mobile phones are a fantastic invention. They make all our lives better. But is being devoted to them an example of being devoted to something worthwhile? We have all witnessed families sitting in a restaurant where everyone is paying attention to their phones and not each other. What would happen to our society if that family in the restaurant put down their phones during that meal? Would the family become weaker? Or would the family become stronger as they engage with each other in conversation? What would happen in our society if families got stronger? Would the chaos of our world increase or decrease?

When writing this section, I spent a day away from home to spend time alone with my thoughts and reflections. I went on a long bike ride in the morning to increase clarity and then drove to the beach to do some writing. I then proceeded to write this section while parked in my car. Want to guess what wasn't with me during this day? Social media apps on my phone. I wanted to spend time devoted to this book and felt that social media would only distract me from the goal of writing words that would help people.

What are you devoted to? And the more difficult question to answer: To what should you be devoted?

The Seven Churches
"John, To the seven churches in the province of Asia." (Revelation 1:4, NIV)

After John has established the legitimacy of his letter and its message, he switches gears and provides the traditional greeting portion of the letter. It would be interesting to go back in time to discover the answer, but we will assume that there are more than seven churches in Asia at this point in time. So, why did John only focus on the seven?

These churches were important because they were on the Roman mail route, the "Cursus Publicus", or the "public way". But why would they be important to the early church? Look at a map of the seven churches:

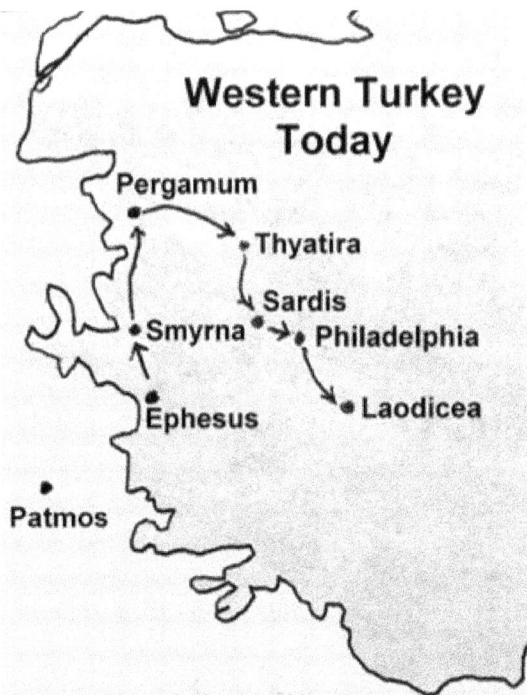

We tend not to believe in coincidences where and when God is involved. As you look at the map, it is probably not a coincidence that the geographical order of the towns matches with the mail route. Basically, John's letter would go to Ephesus because it was the closest to Patmos and was thus also the first church John included in this letters' encouragement to the believers.

The order was no coincidence: God directed the specific order to increase the probability of the letter actually arriving at the churches. This makes sense because if you are going to send a package to a relative, do you think the arrival chances are higher if the package is sent to your aunt in Cincinnati, OH or to your other aunt in Rendville, OH? The mail service infrastructure of people, equipment, and vehicles is greater around Cincinnati than in tiny Rendville which thus increases the potential that your aunt in Cincinnati will receive your letter. The same was true in John's time: because mail would regularly go through Ephesus, Smyrna, etc., the chances of losing the letter was lower than if the letter was sent to a tiny village nestled way up in the mountains.

One other important aspect that bears mention is the concept of a "church" in John's time because it is vastly different from ours. Today our mental picture of a church is a structure where people gather to worship and fellowship. Whether the building is small, large, a campus, a group of believers with multiple locations, or even the beautiful ancient structures, we tend to focus on the building. It hasn't always been like that; the term "church" used to mean the body of believers.

The clearest descriptions of the early church are found in the book of Acts and none of the passages record a church building. On the contrary, the following example depicts the church after it's formation on the Day of Pentecost: "Every day they continued to meet together in the temple courts. They broke bread in their homes and ate together with glad and sincere hearts, praising God and enjoying the favor of all the people. And the Lord added to their number daily those who were being saved." (Acts 2:46-47, NIV). The early church met together without regard for structure. History actually tells us that the early believers met in the members' homes. So, it is important to remember that the seven "churches" were seven bodies of believers and not seven physical buildings with pews, a pulpit, or even a mailbox. More than likely, John's letter was sent to a believer that would have been the focal point of the local body of believers.

"The" not "A"

"And from Jesus Christ, who is the faithful witness, the firstborn from the dead, and the ruler of the kings of the earth" (Revelation 1:5, NIV)

One of the authors (Roger) is a master of over-thinking and reading into things that may or may not be there (although if challenged about it, he will rigorously debate that his analysis is correct and the rest of the world just doesn't see it). Whether this behavior was ingrained into him at a young, impressionable age listening to his father describe the day at the crime lab or absorbed by watching too many police shows on the television may never be known. Perhaps it was gained through osmosis from hanging out with his brother, friends from soccer, or work colleagues who were members of the law enforcement community.

The verse above brings a dilemma to over-thinkers: Is it significant that the text says Jesus is "**The** faithful witness" rather than "**a** faithful witness"? Or is it just thinking too much about the minutiae? Words matter in communication, whether written or verbal. Word choices are important. In general, the use of the definitive article is significant. We worship someone who is **THE** faithful witness for us before a Holy God.

Consider courtroom shows on television. Often witnesses are portrayed in a manner of condemning the accused defendant to punishment. The testimony of witnesses can be circumspect because their intentions are not trustworthy. How cool is it that Jesus is not just a faithful witness, but in fact is the one and only faithful witness for us before a God whose holiness demands perfection from us as well. If the word "**a**" was used in the text, there would be other witnesses when we approach the Throne of God, but we have no need to be concerned with other witnesses.

This was not new subject matter for John. In the second chapter of 1 John we read that "My dear children, I write this to you so that you will not sin. But if anybody does sin, we have one who speaks to the Father in our defense - Jesus Christ, the Righteous One." (1 John 2:1, NIV).

We are grateful for reminders like Revelation 1:5 that Jesus is the only one interceding on our behalf to God. (Jeff's outline of the path to salvation is located in the Bonus section of this book. If you'd like to have Jesus intercede on your behalf by accepting God's gift of salvation, please skip to that section.)

Mourning during the Second Coming?

"'Look, he is coming with the clouds,' and 'every eye will see him, even those who pierced him'; and all peoples on earth 'will mourn because of him.' So shall it be! Amen. 'I am the Alpha and the Omega,' says the Lord God, 'who is, and who was, and who is to come, the Almighty.'" (Revelation 1:7-8, NIV)

Jesus is coming back. We believe this to the core of our being. Will it be today, tomorrow, next week, next year, or even during our lifetimes? We don't know the timing, but are secure in our belief that we will be ready when He comes back.

Verse 7 seems to be written to those who have opted for the path of unbelief. When Jesus comes back, Scripture is quite clear that all people will be judged and the righteous will join God in heaven. It is therefore reasonable to believe that those mourning in verse 7 are those who have made the conscious decision to not follow Jesus.

This seems an odd concept that ALL people will mourn when Jesus comes back. Sure, those condemned to life outside of God, it makes sense.

We realize that at this point in time you may not be a believer. Reading this verse, we would encourage you to consider whether you will rejoice or whether you will mourn when Jesus comes back with the clouds.

Roger's Ramblings: Time Travel

If you could go back in time and change something that would result in a better world, what would it be? Would you go back and be that friend and positive role model to a young man who would eventually turn into a dictator? Would you arm yourself with the medical knowledge to go back and provide a vaccine that would prevent all the deaths from the Great Flu? Would you go back and persuade NASA to continue on with space exploration so that we would have settlements on Mars right now?

What about if you could go back in time and change something about your life? What would you change? Would you pursue a different career path? Would you go back and work up the courage to ask that certain young person in Geometry class out on a date? Or would you go back and get all your money on the Chicago Cubs winning the 2016 World Series? Chances are, if you are like me, there are many things to change in my life that would correct wrong decisions, bad behavior, and poor choices; it would be difficult to narrow this down to only one change.

Our society seems to be obsessed with time travel. The number of books, TV shows, and movies that deal with time travel is incalculable. Numerous television shows such as Quantum Leap, Lost, and Dr. Who come quickly to mind, as do movies such as Back to the Future, Timecop, and the final two Marvel Studios Avenger movies. The time travel topic in these various entertainment mediums have provided enjoyment to millions of people around the world. (Not to mention quite a few discussions about the implications of time travel) For the most part, the overall theme of these has been the need to go back in time to fix a mistake.

Right about now, you're wondering what time travel has to do with the book of Revelation. Let's look at verse 8: "'I am the Alpha and the Omega,' says the Lord God, 'who is, and who was, and who is to come, the Almighty.'" (Revelation 1:8, NIV).

The link between time travel and verse 8 is actually found in the first chapter of the first book of the Bible, Genesis. The four most powerful words in all humanity are found in Genesis 1:1, "In the beginning God". Quite simply, Revelation confirms this truth: God doesn't need to worry about time travel because He is:

- *"The Alpha" - God was present at the beginning of all Creation. In the Greek language, Alpha is the first letter of the alphabet. John's usage of the word conveys that God is the first. It boggles our mind and defies our understanding, but God has always been.*
- *"The Omega" - Just as God has always been, John then goes on to say that He will always be. The word "Omega" is the last word in the Greek alphabet. It was used to convey that God is the "first and the last".*
- *"Who is" - God was the first. He will be the Last. But that wasn't sufficient for John. "He is" is used to assure the early Christians that the same God is present in their lives. And we have assurance that He is with us today.*
- *"And who was" - John is providing us with another descriptor to reinforce that God was present before Creation. Before the dawn of man, God was there.*
- *"And who is to come" - Another point of emphasis that God exists forever.*

Verse 8 speaks to the "omnipresence" of God. So here, it seems appropriate that John uses the phrase "the Almighty" to describe the God that always has been, is today, and will forever be. He has no equal. He is the Almighty.

Would it be cool to go back in time and fix our mistakes? Of course. But what guarantee would we have that the temporary correction will actually fix the mistake in the long term? What if the chain of events would result in a worse condition for us? We all make mistakes; they shape us into the people that we are today. Rather than worrying about changing the future, let's look to the One who has existed throughout time for the path forward.

O Brother...

"I, John, your brother and companion in the suffering and kingdom and patient endurance that are ours in Jesus" (Revelation 1:9, NIV)

John's lament was due to the fact that he was in a similar situation as the early believers, even though he wasn't physically in their midst. He was physically distant, but was also suffering similar to the early believers.

Today, when we are in a similar situation, all we have to do is phone, email, or text that loved one who is far away from us and going through a hard time. Family members of service personnel are intimately familiar with this type of anguish because they are unable to do anything to help alleviate the loneliness or pain. Sending kids to college also falls within this scenario. They're not able to be there with their loved ones in flesh and bones, so their only option is to encourage them through words.

John's description of himself shows the nature of his relationship with the new believers. The word "brother" is translated to mean literally a brother, someone of the same DNA. In fact, it is so clear, that of all the 250+ times it is used in the New Testament, the same Greek word is used. In addition, the Greek for our word "companion" means a co-participant, someone who partakes with you. John then is saying he is their flesh and bone relative who is right there among the same trials and tribulations that the believers are facing.

...Where Art Thou?

"I, John, ...was on the island of Patmos because of the word of God and the testimony of Jesus." (Revelation 1: 9, NIV)

Perhaps no other place mentioned in the New Testament receives as much attention and scrutiny as the island of Patmos. The travels and exploits of Paul, Peter, John, and the other disciples include such towns as Samothrace, Neopolis, Amphipolis, Berea, and Thessalonica. Rarely do you read an article that describes the history of these towns from the first century to modern day. What's interesting is that the above verse is the only instance where the island of Patmos is mentioned in the Bible. What is it about Patmos that entices us to learn more about the island where John had his visions that would form the letter that we today know as the book of Revelation?

Similar to the section on the authorship of the book of Revelation, it is important to fully grasp the conditions that John endured while he was on Patmos.

Introduction to Patmos

Nestled in the northeastern section of the Mediterranean Sea lies a cluster of small islands referred to as the "Dodecanese" island group. These islands are located between the countries of Greece and Turkey in what cartographers classify as the Aegean Sea. Within those clusters of islands lies a small island that was given the name "Patmos" when it was discovered. Learning about Patmos provides contextual footing about John's mindset and his audience in the seven churches of Asia.

Early Patmos

Patmos' formation is steeped in Greek mythology, claiming that the island was on the bottom of the ocean until it was raised to the surface by Zeus. Once the island was above the water and habitable, people began settling on it.

At some point, hundreds of years before the birth of Christ, people in what we now know as Turkey possibly looked west from a beach and decided to launch a boat to explore the unknown. The island is 33 miles (53 kilometers) from Turkey, beyond the visible eye so early explorers didn't know what was out there.

Or perhaps they came from Greece, an even greater distance of approximately 155 miles (250 kilometers) from Athens. Today, with modern technology and transportation, the ferry ride to Patmos is 8 hours from Greece.

The island was in close proximity to the seven churches of Asia to whom John wrote the book of Revelation. While he was exiled on the island, it is natural that his attention and focus could have been on the collection of young churches that were on the mainland.

Patmos Overview

The island itself is relatively small. The total land area is 13 square miles (34 square kilometers), roughly 7 miles (12 km) at its longest point and roughly 6 miles (10 km) at its widest point with a population of roughly 3,000 people. By comparison, the island of Manhattan in New York City is 22 square miles in area and is 12 miles long and 2 miles wide with a population of 1.6 million.

Patmos is described to be steeped with a wide variety of topography - beaches of course, and other areas at sea level, but it is mountainous as well. The tallest point on the island is roughly 880 feet above sea level (270 meters). Photos of Patmos are reminiscent of Catalina Island located off the coast of southern California. Similar to Catalina, there are a couple of main settlements on Patmos.

Most of the population is focused in the village of Hora, which is built around the Monastery of Saint John, one of the largest on the island. The remaining population is scattered in the small villages of Kambos, Groikos, and Skala, which is the main port of the island. Travel is by boat and ferry; Patmos does not have an airport.

The Island of Exiles

At some point during their quest for world domination, the Romans decided that it was necessary to occupy the tiny island of Patmos. As noted previously, life under Roman rule wasn't too bad. As long as you obeyed their laws, paid your taxes, and didn't try to revolt, the Romans left you alone.

But this wasn't the same lifestyle enjoyed by inhabitants of some islands under Roman control which were used as places of banishment for prisoners that they were unable to remove by other methods (eg: killing them). Patmos was designated as such a place of banishment.

Patmos & John

It seems safe to assume that life as an exile on an island wasn't the same as living on a tourist-destination island. Accounts of the living conditions at the time are sparse, but John wasn't sitting by the pool every afternoon working on the book of Revelation while being served fancy adult beverages. He wasn't sent to the island because the Roman government was happy with his involvement with the new sect of

Christianity. John didn't win an "all expenses paid" trip to Patmos on a game show. He was being punished. Life for him, and the other political prisoners that had been sent to Patmos, was difficult.

Roger's Ramblings: Thriving versus Busyness

A popular concept today is that because we are all super busy, we need to draw back on our commitments and focus on ourselves. The theory is that we dilute our effectiveness when we are too busy and spread across too many activities. Between work and commutes, we spend over 40 hours a week on our career. The majority of us also have kids which add many more hours tending to their needs, development, and after-school activities. Many of us also have civic or charitable commitments, including attending and volunteering at church. And of course, prevalent through all of the above is our inability to turn off or put down the mobile communicator we carry everywhere with us. We are busy!

So it's really no wonder why society is telling us to start saying "no" more often. Then we can improve our effectiveness for a select quantity of commitments. The logic is sound: If we are unable to fully focus on specific activities because our thoughts are elsewhere, we should cut down on activities that are less important.

But consider the case of John. Prior to receiving the visions that would lead to the book of Revelation, John's schedule was consistent and likely filled with activity. The Romans wouldn't have allowed the exiles to lounge about throughout the day, enjoying the sunshine and mild weather. The exiles would have been put to hard labor, waking up early in the morning and then working throughout the day, most likely into the evening. Then a little bit of sleep until they woke up and did the exact same thing the next day. They were busy!

John's visions would have had broken up his routine in order to capture the visions by documenting it in writing. His work load for the Romans wouldn't have been reduced; he had to find a way to fit the writing into his schedule.

Back to you. We understand: you're busy. But what in your life needs to be prioritized so that you can make a positive contribution to the lives of others? One of the most important aspects of thriving is the act of stepping outside of yourself to attempt to improve the lives of those around you.

Thriving "amidst the chaos" isn't always for our benefit; many times it requires giving of ourselves: "How can we help others thrive"? Right now, starting today, how can you incorporate reaching out to others to your busy schedule? It doesn't have to be blocking out an hour a day to volunteer at the local homeless shelter. It can be something as simple as spending a few extra minutes talking and listening to an annoying co-worker. It can be something as simple as leaving for work a few minutes early because your neighbor will be outside with their dogs and could use some conversation. Which of us is really too busy to not spend 5 minutes in conversation with someone in our immediate orbit?

Here's the thing about reaching out to others in the midst of our busyness: Focusing on others actually benefits our lives as well. Our mental state improves when we talk and laugh with a neighbor. Human beings are created to bond with other human beings. When we reach out to others, life has a way of creating opportunities for them to reach out to you in the future as well.

Who can you reach out to today in the midst of your busyness?

John: An Eyewitness to Glory

"I turned around to see the voice that was speaking to me. And when I turned I saw seven golden lampstands, and among the lampstands was someone like a son of man, dressed in a robe reaching down to his feet and with a golden sash around his chest. The hair on his head was white like wool, as white as snow, and his eyes were like blazing fire. His feet were like bronze glowing in a furnace, and his voice was like the sound of rushing waters. In his right hand he held seven stars, and coming out of his mouth was a sharp, double-edged sword. His face was like the sun shining in all its brilliance." (Revelation 1:12-16, NIV)

We realize we are "but dust" (Genesis 18:27, NIV) and are thus not conceited enough to think that anything we would write in this section would compare with the glorious sight that John was witness to during this portion of his vision. Read the passage above again and take a minute and reflect on his descriptions of the scene:

- "I saw seven golden lampstands"
- "And among the lampstands was someone like a son of man, dressed in a robe reaching down to his feet"
- "And with a golden sash around his chest"
- "The hair on his head was white like wool"
- "As white as snow"
- "And his eyes were like blazing fire"
- "His feet were like bronze glowing in a furnace"
- "And his voice was like the sound of rushing waters"

- "In his right hand he held seven stars,"
- "And coming out of his mouth was a sharp, double-edged sword."
- "His face was like the sun shining in all its brilliance." (Revelation 1:12-16, NIV)

Wow. John was privy to a sight where he likely struggled for the correct words to describe the awesomeness of the scene. Pay close attention to John's description because he portrays images or sounds that are overwhelming to the senses. In John's day, lampstands were giant objects, not the desk lamps that we consider. Think of how blinding seven lampstands 5-6 feet tall, made entirely of gold would have been to John. The same is true with "white as wool" and "white as snow". Both of us have spent too many years of our lives in northern climates where snow was prevalent during winter. Nothing blinds your eyes quite like stepping outside into a sunny day with snow on the ground. Have you ever been to Niagara Falls or another extra large waterfall? The sound of the rushing water is so tremendous that it is difficult to have conversations in the vicinity of the waterfall. And we often downplay the word "glorious" in our culture today. One reason for this is that we have nothing in our lives with which to compare to the scene John describes. There is no doubt that John was describing the glory of God and Jesus.

In the Presence of God

"When I saw him, I fell at his feet as though dead. Then he placed his right hand on me and said: 'Do not be afraid. I am the First and the Last. I am the Living One; I was dead, and now look, I am alive for ever and ever! And I hold the keys of death and Hades.'" (Revelation 1:17-18, NIV)

Back in the days after man and woman were created, they enjoyed a different relationship with God than we do today. We find a clue to this relationship in Genesis 3:8, "Then the man and his wife heard the sound of the LORD God as he was walking in the garden in the cool of the day, and they hid from the LORD God among the trees of the garden." (NIV) The implication is that Adam, Eve, and God, interacted within the Garden of Eden.

But then this relationship disintegrated. Genesis 3 goes on to tell how sin entered the world through disobedience to God. Once Adam and Eve made the conscious decision to disobey God, and thereby sinned, they were banished from the Garden of Eden (Genesis 3:23). What is significant however is the implication of the text when it describes God walking in the Garden looking for Adam and Eve. The implication of course is that prior to sin, Adam and Eve were able to walk in the Garden WITH God. They enjoyed a relationship, Creator and His creation.

Because of sin, our relationship with God was forever changed. No longer were fallen humans allowed to be upright in the presence of God. The natural response was transformed from a relationship to one of worship and reverence. Notable examples include Abram falling to the ground in response to God in Genesis 17 and Joshua falling to the ground in the presence of God in Joshua 5.

Certain cultures in our world fall to the ground or bow in the presence of royalty. But at the end of the day, these royals are just people that are fallen due to sin. How much greater will the response of people be when they are in the presence of God. It is no wonder then that John, someone who had devoted his entire adult life to telling people about this new religion of Christianity, fell to the ground in the presence of Jesus. This theme will be one to watch as we continue our study of Revelation.

A Directive

"Write, therefore, what you have seen, what is now and what will take place later." (Revelation 1:17-18, NIV)

The directive that guided John to write the letter to the seven churches in Asia was spoken none other than by Jesus. We can't count the number of times that we have ignored commands or directives from employees, family members, spouses, etc. Hundreds, possibly even thousands!

But none of us have been commanded to do something directly by Jesus as John was during his visions. All of us are eternally grateful that John didn't ignore this directive!

Seven Angels, Seven Churches...the Start of Symbolism

"The seven stars are the angels of the seven churches, and the seven lampstands are the seven churches." (Revelation 1:20, NIV)

The book of Revelation is full of symbolism and can be confusing. Sometimes the meaning is obvious, sometimes understandable, and sometimes it will remain unclear until the second coming of Jesus. We encourage you to avoid getting hung up on symbolism as you read through the book.

Take verse 20 for example. John provides an answer for what the seven lampstands represent: they represent the seven churches in the province of Asia. Thus, the meaning of this passage of Scripture is that God is walking amongst the churches. This would have been welcome news to the believers because they could take comfort in being in the presence of God.

Then there is the matter of the seven stars. John tells us that the seven stars are the seven angels of the seven churches. Huh? What exactly is an angel of a church? Unfortunately John doesn't provide that answer to us in the text.

Of course, there have been many theories throughout time. One interpretation of the meaning is the angels are heavenly beings. Another interpretation is that the angels are the actual human leaders of the gathering of the believers in that city. Another interpretation is that there are actually heavenly beings acting as guardians to the churches. If this interpretation is correct, that there are angels guarding churches, does this carry on to today? There was an interesting fictional book written back in the 1980's about the spiritual warfare between angels and demons that might be worth reading if you have the time. The book is called *"This Present Darkness"*, written by Frank E. Peretti.

The answer to the question of what are the seven angels is this: We simply don't know. But regardless of the various interpretations, one thing is clear: There will be passages in the book of Revelation where we will not have an answer for the meaning of the symbolism used by John. Our goal is to focus on the big picture and themes of Revelation, particularly how we can learn lessons from the book to improve our lives in our world today.

Dig Deeper: Questions to Consider

We've covered a lot of ground and information whilst learning about the first chapter in Revelation. How are you doing with this level of information? Excited for the remainder of the book? Overwhelmed by the content of the first book of Revelation?

We encourage you to buckle-up. The next few chapters focus specifically on John's message to each of the seven churches in Asia. We firmly believe that the content for those churches was not only relevant to the believers during John's time, but it is relevant for us today as well.

Before you head to the next chapter, let's focus on applying what we learned in this chapter. Consider the following questions:

1. How is your life blessed? Actually write a list and review the list for a week. Spend time thanking God for those blessings.

2. What would be the most desirable item in your life that you would change if you could go back in time? How would your life be different today?

3. Why was it important for John to focus on the omnipresence of God?

4. Close your eyes while someone else reads aloud verses 12-16 to you or use an audible version of the Bible. Describe what you see in your mind as to what John describes.

5. Is it important to completely understand all of the symbolism found in the book of Revelation? Why? Why not?

Ephesus

Revelation Chapters 2 & 3 Overview

Jesus Speaks:

These two chapters set the stage for the remainder of Revelation as to the distinction between the author and the source of the message. John was the author; he was the person that received Jesus's vision and subsequently wrote the letters to the seven churches.

Jesus however was the speaker of the words that John directly recorded into the letters and was the source of the inspiration for the letter text not directly attributed to Jesus. Many Bibles have Jesus's words printed in red-letter and there are many passages in Revelation that are colored red. These two chapters are nearly exclusively colored red because they are the exact words spoken by Jesus.

As you continue reading, we attribute authorship to Jesus and John as the message-deliverer.

Chapter Structure:

The best method to approach the next two chapters is to consider each section as an individual letter written to each of the seven churches. Starting with the church in Ephesus, chapters 2 and 3 include a total of seven letters.

Structure of the Letter to the Churches:

The structures of the letters are similar to each other. John starts by providing the description of Jesus in the vision to establish Him as the ultimate writer of the letter. John then records Jesus's recognition of something good that the believers are doing. But after building them up with congratulations, Jesus then proceeds to admonish the churches for what could be improved. John then concludes the letter with Jesus's words reminding the believers of what their reward will be if they correct that poor behavior.

Description of Jesus:

The prevalent perception in our society is a loving, peaceful Jesus. Does Jesus love everyone? Absolutely. Does He desire that every human being come into an eternal relationship with Him? You betcha. But is He timid like a church mouse? Absolutely not. Quite the opposite actually. Read the descriptions that John uses in chapters 2 & 3; what image comes to mind?

- Church in Ephesus: "the words of him who holds the seven stars in his right hand and walks among the seven golden lampstands." (Revelation 2:1, NIV)
- Smyrna: "the words of him who is the First and the Last, who died and came to life again." (Revelation 2:8, NIV)
- Pergamum: "the words of him who has the sharp, double-edged sword" (Revelation 2:12, NIV)
- Thyatira: "the words of the Son of God, whose eyes are like blazing fire and whose feet are like burnished bronze." (Revelation 2:18, NIV)
- Sardis: "the words of him who holds the seven spirits of God and the seven stars." (Revelation 3:1, NIV)
- Philadelphia: "the words of him who is holy and true, who holds the key of David. What he opens no one can shut, and what he shuts no one can open." (Revelation 3:7, NIV).
- Laodicea: "the words of the Amen, the faithful and true witness, the ruler of God's creation." (Revelation 3:14, NIV)

It is no wonder that Jesus used this strong language in these letters; He wanted to remind the early believers that they worshiped and followed a strong God, one who was powerful enough to aid them throughout their struggles amidst persecution from Rome. This message is the same for us today.

Another reason for John to remind the churches that the authorship of the letter was from Jesus is because the message was going to be difficult for the believers to hear. Instruction was coming.

Good Job!

Basic management doctrine encourages leaders to build up people before engaging in difficult conversations. Think of some of your annual job performance reviews. Did your manager start the conversation by telling you all of the items you need to improve? Probably not. If they are remotely effective as a manager, the first thing they did was review all of your positive actions and contributions that you delivered to the business. In other words, they built you up.

It could be said that Jesus may have been employing the same technique in the message to John. He had words of encouragement for most of the churches. The encouragement varies from church to church as we will discuss later in this chapter. But, He was able to find positive aspects and give the churches praise.

But there's a problem you need to fix....

John wrote the letters many hundreds of years ago so we can only guess at the response of the churches to the admonishments they received in their letter. If human nature was the same back then as it is today, they quite likely began making excuses for their poor behavior. We can hear the believers in Ephesus say, "It's not our fault that we have fallen a little bit from our excitement at living a Christian lifestyle when we became believers. We received no further instruction from you. If you think about it, it's really your fault for not responding to our pleas." Does this attitude sound familiar?

It's interesting to us that while the majority of the churches received praise, all but one of the churches was encouraged to work and improve some aspect of their behavior. Because the instructions were different to each church, these will also be discussed in the specific church section.

Here are some ideas to help you fix your problem....

Jesus wasn't like the teacher who sent a student's failing report card to their parents without any explanation or ideas about how to improve. No, after identifying the problem with the specific body of believers, He offered advice on how they could resolve the problem and then move forward. As you might imagine, this is different for each church.

<u>Fixing the problem will lead to a reward!</u>

We will also spend time detailing the reward Jesus mentioned for each specific church, but here is a spoiler: Heaven and eternal life!

Let's dive in and start with the first church, Ephesus.

Background of Ephesus

Unless you are a regular church-goer, it is safe to say that you've probably never heard of Ephesus. Despite being a major city back in the first century, Ephesus does not exist as a city today. This is curious because it was an important city, a leader in commerce, a focal point for Roman spirituality, and a city where prosperity drove cultural renaissance.

Nestled on the east side of a bay on the east side of the Aegean Sea, the city of Ephesus was one of the most important cities at the time of John's writing. Strategically located amongst the outlet of the Cayster River to the Aegean Sea, the location was quite desirable. Traders and merchants were able to send goods by the Aegean Sea, up the Cayster River, or on land routes. Think of modern-day Portland, Oregon: ships from Asia deliver goods to the port by coming in on the Columbia River, but there are also boats from the east portion of the Columbia bringing goods to Portland as well. Long-haul trucks utilize many routes, most notably Interstate 5, to bring goods over the land into Portland also. Likewise, several trade routes passed through Ephesus, which increased the wealth of the inhabitants.

Cities that are well-off commercially tend to also be strong culturally as well. Think here of a parallel with large cities around the world that have strong commercial industries. New York City is arguably one of the most prosperous cities in the world. It is also thereby a leading city in music, theater, and other art pursuits. The city of Ephesus enjoyed a similar position during the time of John. The library in the city, the Library of Celsus, boasted a book inventory that was without equal in the area of Asia. The arts were so important to the Ephesians that they built a 24,000 seat theater for artistic performances. That's the size of a modern day basketball/hockey arena!

Home to the temple of Artemis, the Greek goddess of hunting, wilderness, animals, and childbirth, Ephesus was also a religious center. The worship of Artemis was so strong in fact, that it impacted the commercial viability of Ephesus. The prosperity of countless Ephesians depended upon people continuing to engage in worship of Artemis through statues and other trinkets.

Taken together, it becomes clear of the challenges the church in Ephesus faced in the first century. Yes, they were a strong, established church, but there were many obstacles to maintaining their faith and achieving growth while following Jesus.

Formation of the Church in Ephesus

By the time that John wrote Revelation, the church in Ephesus had been in existence for 40+ years. The church is first mentioned in the 18th chapter of the book of Acts. In total, there are 18 references to the church in Ephesus throughout the remainder of the New Testament. It is widely believed that the church was formed at some point during Pauls' early missionary journeys.

But Paul didn't just start the church and move on to another church in another city, never to step foot again in Ephesus. Paul also went on to spend approximately two years in Ephesus from 52-54 AD, primarily preaching the Gospel and building up the new church in the city that was a fertile ground for new followers of Christ.

The importance of the church in Ephesus is further demonstrated in that Paul wrote a letter to the church around 60 AD. This letter is what we know as the book of Ephesians in the New Testament. The first half of the letter was focused on strengthening the foundations of their faith while the second half of the letter provided guidance for living holy in their culture.

The early leaders of Christianity spent much time and effort building up the church in Ephesus, so if there ever was a church that didn't need encouragement and correction, you would think it would be the church in Ephesus. But despite all of that work and effort, something between the years of 60 AD to 90 AD created situations within the church that required special counsel. Why is this?

Roger's Ramblings: Being Comfortable Is Not the Same as Thriving

The key to understanding the position of the church in 90 AD can actually be found in the 18th, 19th, and 20th chapters of Acts. When Paul and his team of missionaries first arrived in Ephesus, they found a city that had no experience or preconceptions about how to follow Jesus's ways. The nineteenth verse of Acts 18 reads, "They [Paul, etc.) arrived at Ephesus, where Paul left Priscilla and Aquila. He himself went into the synagogue and reasoned with the Jews. When they asked him to spend more time with them..." (Acts 18:19, NIV).

Ephesus was fertile soil and Christianity increased substantially as we read the following in the 19th chapter: "Paul entered the synagogue and spoke boldly there for three months, arguing persuasively about the kingdom of God. But some of them became obstinate; they refused to believe and publicly maligned the Way. So Paul left them. He took the disciples with him and had discussions daily in the lecture hall of Tyrannus. This went on for two years, so that all the Jews and Greeks who lived in the province of Asia heard the word of the Lord." (Acts 19:8-10, NIV).

At some point, the number of people open to the Gospel had reached a saturation point and opportunities to obtain new converts were few and far between. The non-believers were more interested in their prosperity on earth rather than following the ways of Jesus, which taught ever-lasting prosperity in heaven. Chapters 19 & 20 go on to describe the turmoil that gripped the city as the non-believers violently objected to the new believers. Imagine being a new believer in a city where your neighbors objected to your beliefs so strongly that riots occurred. If the riots and other opposition to the new religion were at the time when Paul was in Ephesus, the church continued to function for the next 40+ years.

Which brings us to the lesson with the church in Ephesus. Given the strong adherence to a high level of prosperity, much of which came from promoting Artemis, did the believers stand firm on their principles and become a counter-influence? Or did they seek to operate at "peace" with the outside world? By operating in the largest city in Asia, did they become comfortable and forget their reliance on God? The fact that Jesus had things to say to Ephesus seems to answer those questions.

There is a saying in our culture which may have resonated with the members of the church in Ephesus: "We're kind of a big deal". You may have even said this yourself from time to time. Your team won the over-40 basketball league and someone posts "We're kind of a big deal" on social media. You tune into a television quiz show and answer 80% of the questions correctly? You're kind of a big deal.

The problem with thinking that you're a big deal is that it tends to negate work towards improvement. Being good at something is akin to the prosperity of the Ephesian people. Experience tells us that prosperity leads to being comfortable, which in turn leads to laziness.

An example from my life: After college, I moved away from my friends and back to my hometown. I missed playing soccer and looked for opportunities to play again. One Sunday afternoon, I saw a dozen or so men playing soccer in a local park, introduced myself, and joined them. Turns out they were all either medical students or doctors. The next week I went back and played. And the next week. And the next. They were all very good and I continually was challenged to improve my skills. From there, I started playing in the city-wide outdoor 11 v 11 league, numerous indoor leagues, smaller field outdoor leagues, and countless evenings of open play. Having never played soccer in high school or college, I wasn't the best player, but I certainly wasn't the worst either. As long as I made the effort to keep improving, there were few times when I embarrassed myself.

But something happened along the way. Thinking that I was good enough, I stopped working on my footwork. I stopped working on my speed and endurance. I stopped working on passing to my teammates. In other words, in my mind at least, I became "a big deal." When I played goalie, I gave up puff goals but blamed the defense. When I played striker and missed scoring a goal, it wasn't my fault, it was someone else's fault. My teammates didn't make a good pass to me. Or they passed too late. It was never my fault. I got comfortable and my game suffered.

Do you know any churches today that fall within this thought process? They can be the biggest church in the area, with thousands of people attending every week and thousands more watching on-line. They are likely to face the temptation of being comfortable.

How about you? Do you fall within this thought process in some area of your life? Have you stopped learning and furthering your education? Have you stopped focusing on improving your health? Have you stopped improving your spiritual walk with Jesus?

For human beings, thriving requires constant improvement. If there is one lesson we can learn from the church in Ephesus, let us learn to not be comfortable. We need to continue improving our lives and impact on this earth. We need to continue to focus on others.

In other words, you need to put a note on your bathroom mirror that says, "You are not a big deal. But your God is a big deal."

Good Job!

Do not misunderstand us: the church in Ephesus had a lot going for it. Look at the level of praise that Jesus gives the Ephesians: "I know your deeds, your hard work and your perseverance. I know that you cannot tolerate wicked people, that you have tested those who claim to be apostles but are not, and have found them false. You have persevered and have endured hardships for my name, and have not grown weary." (Revelation 2:2-3, NIV).

Being believers in a hostile environment is a challenge and it sounds like the Ephesians were up to the challenge: their deeds were good. Their hard work was good. And their perseverance, arguably the most challenging aspect of their faith, was commendable. Later in verse three, John again speaks to their perseverance and their ability to continue on in the face of hardships from a culture that worshiped a Greek goddess.

The phrase, "Testing those who claim to be apostles but are not" sounds like it could have been written for believers in our society today. There have always been people who claimed to speak for God throughout history. But it seems like the number of such false prophets have dramatically increased over recent decades, probably due to the increase of media impact on our culture, including the Internet. It can be tricky for people to know what is truth and what is not truth. We would do well to learn from the Ephesians' example.

Unfortunately, all was not great with the church in Ephesus though, because the next passage spoke to the challenges that the church was experiencing.

But we need to talk about...

"Yet I hold this against you: You have forsaken the love you had at first." (Revelation 2:4, NIV).

This is going to be the easiest section of the required corrections out of all the seven churches. Every one reading this book has heard at some point in their lives that in order for love to succeed, it has to be worked at. Long-term marriages do not happen by chance; both partners make a commitment to work hard on a constant basis to make the love stronger.

We will never know for sure what happened with the Ephesian church, but it seems clear that at some point the believers stopped working on improving their new faith and their relationship with Jesus and God. Perhaps they stopped learning about the scriptures to learn how it applied to their lives. Perhaps they listened to the scriptures being spoken about during their meetings, but didn't actually do the next, and all important, step of applying it to their lives. Perhaps individually they stopped meeting with the group of believers. Perhaps they stopped praying.

Ultimately it doesn't matter what happened with the believers in Ephesus. What matters is the condition of your heart and your faith. Are you working at it, improving your life? Or have you gotten comfortable, started slacking off, and have forsaken your love for God?

Repent!!

"Consider how far you have fallen! Repent and do the things you did at first. If you do not repent, I will come to you and remove your lampstand from its place." (Revelation 2:5, NIV).

Perhaps no other word in the Bible is filled with as much promise as the word written twice in verse 5. The word "repent" plays such an important role in God's plan that John uses it ten times in the book of Revelation. As you would imagine, most of the instances are recorded in the first three chapters, the letters to the churches.

According to Webster's, the modern day definition of the word "repent" means, "to turn from sin and dedicate oneself to the amendment of one's life." Using this definition to further refine verse 5 brings clarity to John's message to the Ephesians. The implication is that if the believers don't "turn from their sin and dedicate themselves to the amendment of their lives", there will be consequences. Namely that Jesus will no longer be a part of the church, and without Jesus, life eternal might also no longer be possible.

John's letter reminded the early believers that it was possible to get right with God if they turned away from their sin. Were they skipping meeting together? They needed to repent. Were they not standing up for God amongst the people of Ephesus? They needed to repent. Were they straying and engaging in the worship of Artemis?

They needed to repent.

Repentance was key for the Ephesians and it is key for us today as well. Is there something in your life where you have fallen? Repent.

But Also Good Job

"But you have this in your favor: You hate the practices of the Nicolaitans, which I also hate." (Revelation 2:6, NIV)

After praising the believers and then bringing them back down to earth with corrections, Jesus bestows additional praise on the believers in Ephesus. This won't be the last time that we read of the practices of the Nicolaitans: apparently the church in Pergamum was unable to hate their practices. What were the practices of the Nicolaitans? The scholarly consensus is that the Nicolaitans engaged in immorality. Jeff provides a good synopsis in his Points to Ponder at the end of this chapter.

But let's not lose sight of the real takeaway from this verse as we seek to thrive in the chaos of our society. The key to thriving found in this verse is simple: Hate what God hates, love what God loves.

"Call to Action"

"Whoever has ears, let them hear what the Spirit says to the churches..." (Revelation 2:7, NIV)

This phrase, although short and seemingly insignificant, is found in each of the letters that were written to the seven churches in Asia. This is interesting as we think back to one of the questions we posed earlier in this book: Were the letters specifically delivered to only the church in question or did all seven churches get to read the dirty laundry of the other churches. If all seven letters were distributed to each of the churches, one would think that including this phrase in the introductory part of the letter (IE: chapter 1) would have been sufficient instead of repeating the phrase seven times. This seems to support the theory that each letter was only sent to the corresponding church.

But not necessarily. This phrase is so powerful that it is entirely plausible that the message needed to be repeated multiple times. It's only thirteen or so words, you might be saying; is it really that powerful? The answer is unequivocally, Yes. Within this short passage we find a command, a call to action, and a bridge to a promise.

The Command:

The reader is commanded to pay attention to what is written in the letter. At some point in our lives, we have all been guilty of passively listening when someone has been talking to us. We say we're listening but we're really focusing on the movie, football game on TV, our mounting to-do list, or not dying in the video game. It seems safe to assume that this condition has plagued humans since the dawn of creation. John didn't want the believers that read or heard the letter to not act upon the commands in the letter. They were to do what it said.

There is also a concept about awareness and ignorance: once we are aware of something, we are compelled to act and do what is required; we cannot claim ignorance. Good Samaritan laws are a good example of this concept: if we are in a situation where we can assist someone in need, we are legally required to provide the appropriate level of action. This is also a legal concept: If we are aware of something bad happening and do nothing to report it, we are complicit in the illegal activity. Once the believer in Ephesus read the letter or had the letter read to them during a church gathering, they were compelled to act upon the commands included in the letter.

The Call to Action:

John expected active, not passive, listening. The instructions included in the various letters were of extreme importance and required action. For Ephesus, they needed to radically change their thinking and get back into the habit of placing God first in their lives. Whenever there is a clear call to action in the Bible, it is always a good idea to pay attention and do what it says. To reinforce this point, John again includes a reference that the letters didn't originate with him, the letters were of divine origin.

Another interesting point is the audience of the call to action. Notice that John didn't address the call to action to the ministers or the church leaders. No. The instructions in the letter were to be followed by everyone that possessed ears. Which, save for a tiny minority of people, includes every human being.

The Bridge to a Promise:

The most exciting part of this seemingly insignificant phrase is that it bridges from an action to a promise. The believers were told that if they do what the letter commands, then they will be rewarded. In the case of the Ephesians, if they renewed their faith with God, then their reward would be life eternal. As we study the other churches, pay special attention to their promised reward.

The Reward

"To the one who is victorious, I will give the right to eat from the tree of life, which is in the paradise of God." (Revelation 2:7, NIV)

Let's recap the church in Ephesus as we wrap up this first section of chapter 2. One of the earliest churches started to follow the ways of Christ, it had grown to be one of the most significant and prestigious. It appears that the believers felt good about themselves because they were able to maintain a presence in a city that, for the most part, had a completely different set of beliefs. But, they were probably too proud of themselves and started drifting away from God and the intent behind their original formation. So God, in His infinite kindness, sent an encouragement for them to revert back to their faith. The letter reminded them that if they repent, they could experience the reward, but if they didn't repent, then there would be consequences.

The reward? It wasn't a surprise: eternal life! The usage of the phrase "tree of life" would have resonated with believers that were familiar with what we know as the Old Testament. The promised reward to the believers in Ephesus was quite simple: Repent and live with God forever.

This promise was not inclusive only to the believers in Ephesus. It remains available to us today. Repent and we will live with God forever.

Points to Ponder with Jeff: Keeping Your First Love

Can you think of something that you used to love but you are no longer passionate about? I used to be a big fan of the Chicago Bears. Every chance I had I would watch them on TV. I even went to one of their pre-season games at the old Chicago field. I knew who the key players were. I loved watching Walter Payton run the ball. I remember cheering them on when they won the 1985 Super Bowl. But now I am not really interested in them. I don't know their record. I don't know their players. I really don't know much about them. What happened? Slowly, over time, as players changed, I moved away from Illinois and started watching other teams. I didn't wake up one morning and thought, "I no longer am a Bears fan". It just happened. Some would say that I "lost my love" for the "Da Bears."

Losing the love for a sports team really won't make a difference in the light of eternity but there is something that will make a difference for eternity – our love for God. The first message we find in the book of Revelation contains a major problem – they had "lost their first love". Could it happen today? Does it happen today? The answer to both is "Yes". What can we do to keep it from happening? Read the words to the first church addressed in Revelation and you can find some answers.

"To the angel of the church in Ephesus write: These are the words of him who holds the seven stars in his right hand and walks among the seven golden lampstands: I know your deeds, your hard work and your perseverance. I know that you cannot tolerate wicked men, that you have tested those who claim to be apostles but are not, and have found them false. You have persevered and have endured hardships for my name, and have not grown weary. Yet I hold this against you: You have forsaken your first love. Remember the height from which you have fallen! Repent and do the things you did at first. If you do not repent, I will come to you and remove your lampstand from its place. But you have this in your favor: You hate the practices of the Nicolaitans, which I also hate. He who has an ear, let him hear what the Spirit says to the churches. To him who overcomes, I will give the right to eat from the tree of life, which is in the paradise of God." (Revelation 2:1-7, NIV)

Point #1: Give Jesus the place He deserves in your life. (Verse 1)

Verse one paints an amazing picture. The imagery of Jesus from Revelation 1 is carried into the message to Ephesus and into the letters to the other churches in Asia. It is a picture of authority. It is a picture of connection. It is a picture of power. It is that picture of Jesus that we need to have of Jesus in our own life.

When we face problems in life a lot of different things go through our mind. We might focus on who caused the problem or what caused the problem. We might focus on who we could blame for the problem! Whatever we focus on we usually find ourself in the middle of the issue and try to figure out what we can do.

John's opening words here have a subtle message that I think we need to acknowledge. Instead of making us the center of coming up with a solution, give Jesus the proper place – He is the one with authority, He is the one with power.

I had a gentleman come up to me one time and say, "Could you put my wife on that sick/prayer list? We've tried everything else so we might as well try that." In other words, Jesus wasn't first, He was at the bottom of the list. The next time you find your life in chaos – give Jesus His proper place. Go to Him first.

Point #2: Persevere and Work Hard at your faith. (Verses 2-3)

Sometimes the image is given that when you become a Christian all your problems will go away and you will never have another bad day in your life. The problem with that is that Jesus never promised that the Christian life was always going to be easy. In fact, He says it is going to be tough at times.

He recognized what the Ephesian believers were going through. The church had to be on guard for false teachers. There were some that were even claiming to be "apostles". They put them to the test and determined that they were not to be followed. They were also probably facing forms of persecution for their faith. We know from the book of Acts that Paul was publicly accused and put on trial for his faith. What does Jesus notice about the church at Ephesus? They persevered and worked hard to retain their faith.

Could Jesus say the same thing to you that He said to the Ephesian church? "You have persevered and have endured hardships for my name, and have not grown weary." We probably all want to say, "I hope so!" We want Jesus's approval. We want Him to be proud of us. The reality is – it is going to take some hard work and perseverance on our part. This is especially true when facing turmoil in life. The example of the Ephesians is an example we need to follow. Hang in there! Jesus knows what you are going through.

Point #3: Be honest about your relationship with God. (Verses 4-5)

When the people in the church of Ephesus first heard these words read I wonder how many of them said, "You nailed it, Jesus! That is exactly where I am at right now. I was just getting ready to repent!" My guess is that none of them said that. In fact, they may have been taken back and even insulted a little. But Jesus was just being honest with them.

A true sign of love is that someone shares with you what you need to hear, not what you want to hear. If you have a friend like that it is a special friendship. Being brutally honest is sometimes hard but if done out of love the goal is restoration, not condemnation.

Jesus cared for them and He cares for us. He doesn't want us to lose the spark in our eye or the excitement in our heart that we had when we first came to Him. Why? Because He wants you with Him for eternity.

There's just one more thing. If that relationship is not where it needs to be in your life He tells you what you need to do – Repent. Of what? Only you may know, but it is worth it.

Point #4: Don't give in to the cultural norm. (Verse 6)

We don't know a lot about the Nicolaitans but obviously Jesus didn't agree with them. What we do know is that they were a group of people that lived by the philosophy of sexual promiscuity. They seemed to rationalize that they had been "freed" from the Mosaic law through the sacrifice of Christ and that they had no restrictions on their sexual behavior.

Whatever the exact sins of the Nicolaitans were, it is obvious that Jesus expected His followers not to fall into their ranks. He commends the Christians in Ephesus for not buying into their philosophy and practices.

We learn from Jesus words that we need to have standards and take a stand for what is right. It is rather obvious in our culture today that sexual promiscuity is the accepted norm. You don't have to watch TV long or go to very many movies to find a pervading philosophy that sexual expression does not follow Biblical standards.

Jesus expects those who follow Him to follow the standards of purity and holiness. Chaos and turmoil are found in the lives of too many families and even churches where Christians seemed to accept the cultural norm instead of the Biblical standard.

Point #5: Live for the promises of God. (Verse 7)

Do you want to live a blessed life? Do you want to receive the promises of God? Then listen to what Jesus tells you. At the end of every message that Jesus delivers to the churches in Revelation you will find a command to hear what the spirit says to the churches. You would think that something like that would not have to be said, but it was. And because it was written and recorded in Revelation, we are provided a path to living a blessed life.

The blessing that Jesus promises here is an amazing statement. The right to eat from the "tree of life" is something that has been banned for man from the beginning of time. It was the "tree of life" in Genesis 3 that God made impossible for man to partake of. After Adam and Eve sinned by eating from the tree of "knowledge of good and evil" God blocked access to the tree of life.

The amazing promise of access to that tree is one that should not be taken lightly. It is offered to those who listen to what Jesus is telling them. I want to encourage you to receive the blessings God offers. If you are not where you were at one time in your walk with God, if you have let chaos dominate your heart and life, if you have "lost your first love", come back and claim the promises of God. He wants you to live with Him forever in heaven. Don't turn your back on the promises He offers.

Smyrna

Background on Smyrna

If you were to visit Western Turkey today you could go to the city of Ismir and be at the site of the ancient city of Smyrna. It was a city founded in the 11th century BC and flourished for a while but then basically died out. It was resurrected and restored when Alexander the Great swept through the known world in the 4th century BC. In verse 8 Jesus uses this imagery of being dead and then resurrected to immediately connect with the historical culture of the Christians who lived in that city.

The people of Smyrna were real people, living out their daily lives and were trying their best to follow Jesus in a world that opposes what they believed. Their biggest direct opposition came not from the Roman government, but from a group that Jesus also had some issues with – the Jews. The Jews were the biggest threat to the followers of Christ because they could be informers against them to the Roman government.

Second Thoughts on the Angels of the Churches

"Write this letter to the angel of the church in Smyrna..." (Revelation 2:8, NIV)

Each of the seven letters starts with a command from Jesus to John to write a letter to the "angel" of the church. Earlier we discussed whether these were actually angels (spiritual beings) or someone in a leadership position of the church. The word here literally means a messenger, so it is probable that the letters were intended for the human leader of the churches.

Which of course sounds obvious, right? But it does bring up an interesting thought: would John be able to ensure that the letter was delivered to all of the believers? One of the criticisms of the early church was that until the Renaissance the person in leadership was tasked with the reading of scripture to the congregation. Humans, even people in leadership positions, are subject to sinful behavior and there were many instances where the leader twisted the scripture for their own benefit. How would they get caught because the majority of the congregation couldn't read the language of the Bible (Latin)?

Were the leaders of the seven churches in Asia similarly tempted? Take Ephesus for example: It would have been no problem at all for the leader ("angel") of the church to take the letter, crumple it up, and file it in File 13 (trash can). But to their credit, the leaders withstood the temptation which is why we have the book of Revelation today.

The lesson to us today? Do the right thing even if it is uncomfortable. Especially if it is uncomfortable. You never know how it will impact people in the future.

Jesus is the Author

"...These are the words of him who is the First and the Last, who died and came to life again." (Revelation 2:8-11, NIV)

Even though the imagery of being dead and alive connects with the people in Smyrna, it is obvious that there is more to that imagery. The First and the Last, who was dead but is now alive – Who is this referring to? Jesus. See, you are already beginning to understand the use of symbolic language and imagery. It obviously refers to His resurrection and the "First and Last" phrase is consistently used in the book of Revelation to refer to Jesus. Jesus himself gives us the imagery in chapter one Rev 1:17-18 - "Do not be afraid. I am the First and the Last. I am the Living One; I was dead, and behold I am alive for ever and ever!

What follows then are the words of Jesus to the Christians in Smyrna. Unlike the message to the Ephesian church and four of the other churches in the list, there is not a reference to wrong doing or a problem they have. This is only true of the church at Smyrna and Philadelphia.

There are No Secrets

"I know your afflictions and your poverty - yet you are rich! I know about the slander of those who say they are Jews and are not, but are a synagogue of satan." (Revelation 2:9, NIV)

Smyrna was known as a wealthy city. So why would he say they were suffering and poor? Two possible reasons. First, if they had left the Jewish faith and had been employed by fellow Jews, they would have been cast out and probably have lost their jobs. Second, in the Roman culture you almost always had to be a part of a Roman trade guild and most of those guilds required their members to participate in the pagan activities and sacrifices. Those Christians whose lives were changed could no longer participate in such activities.

Why does Jesus then say they are rich? He does not see things from an earthly or material perspective. He didn't look at bank accounts or homes or cars, He looked at the human heart. This is an amazing compliment to the Christians – they were indeed rich because of the blessings they shared in Christ. Jesus goes on then and addresses the suffering they were facing.

Beware: Suffering is Coming

"Do not be afraid of what you are about to suffer. I tell you, the devil will put some of you in prison to test you, and you will suffer persecution for ten days. Be faithful, even to the point of death, and I will give you life as your victor's crown." (Revelation 2:10, NIV)

Smyrna was a city that was known for being very loyal to Rome and the Roman leaders. If you wanted to get someone in trouble all you had to do was inform a Roman official of anything that might be considered an offense against Rome and the officials would respond. By the time of John, it is attested that Christians in Asia Minor were generally charged with treason if accused by such "informers". The Jews in Smyrna were reportedly fulfilling the function of "informers" by simply claiming publicly that Christians were no longer welcome as part of the "synagogue community", a form of betrayal. The Roman law allowed the Jewish faith and places of worship – the synagogue -

to exist but Christians who were not seen as Jewish had no protection against the Roman law which required worship of the Roman Emperor Domitian. If someone was accused of going against this they were given a chance to renounce their faith and pay homage to Caesar. If they refused, there would be consequences to face.

Jesus goes right to the real source of the problem: satan is the one behind it all. The Jews would accuse the Christians and lie about them. This is what Jesus said of them when He dealt with them in John 8: "You belong to your father, the devil, and you want to carry out your father's desire. He was a murderer from the beginning, not holding to the truth, for there is no truth in him. When he lies, he speaks his native language, for he is a liar and the father of lies." (John 8:44-45, NIV)

How about today? Is there suffering in our world today?

These are rhetorical questions because of course there is suffering in our world today. The father of lies has continued to operate in our world throughout history, from the time of Jesus until today. One only has to turn on the nightly news to see all of the suffering that exists in our world. What's even more horrifying to consider is that the suffering we see on the evening news has been hand-selected as the worst-of-the-worst suffering. There is more suffering out there! A ton of it! Yes, we know suffering will come. It's already here! Some people are suffering more than others, but we all suffer in this fallen and broken world. Many people around the world are suffering solely for their faith.

But the real question for us as we seek to thrive in today's culture is how we will respond when we are suffering. One only has to do a quick study on the life of Paul to see how he responded to suffering. Take his letter to the Colossians for example:

"Now I rejoice in what I am suffering for you, and I fill up in my flesh what is still lacking in regard to Christ's afflictions, for the sake of his body, which is the church. I have become its servant by the commission God gave me to present to you the word of God in its fullness— the mystery that has been kept hidden for ages and generations, but is now disclosed to the Lord's people. To them God has chosen to make known among the Gentiles the glorious riches of this mystery, which is Christ in you, the hope of glory.

He is the one we proclaim, admonishing and teaching everyone with all wisdom, so that we may present everyone fully mature in Christ. To this end I strenuously contend with all the energy Christ so powerfully works in me." (Colossians 1:24-29, NIV)

Persecution Today?

On first glance, this section seems at odds with the theme of this book of gleaning ideas from the book of Revelation as to how to thrive amidst the chaos of modern life. But in reality, this section is necessary because persecution wasn't just something that happened during the time of John and the early church. Persecution against believers and the church was something that has occurred throughout history and is happening today.

Would it surprise you to learn that the level of persecution against the global church today is greater than at any other time in history? It certainly surprised us while we were researching this book. According to the 2023 "World Watch List Report" by the Open Doors organization, well over 300 million Christians in the world "suffer high levels of persecution and discrimination for their faith". This sounds like a huge number because it is: 300 million translates to 1 in every 7 Christians are being persecuted. One in 7. (Note: the link to this report is found in the Notes section of this book).

More than likely, you are like us and don't dwell on this level of persecution because it is happening thousands of miles away in countries in Asia and Africa. The persecution doesn't affect our daily lives so we push it to the back of our mind. Besides, we tell ourselves, we live in a tolerant society, one where persecution will never rear it's ugly head.

Much is being written and debated on "Christian social media" as to whether the church is in decline and losing it's relevance in society today. The impact on our ability to thrive is that the further society progresses away from Biblical standards and morals, the greater the divide between those who believe and those who do not believe. History teaches us that the greater a divide between groups of people, the higher the propensity for a loss of respect between the groups. This loss of respect breeds discord, which leads to hate, which leads to persecution.

Our point here is for you to consider your response to persecution should it manifest itself during our time on this earth. What should our response be as believers to persecution against us or other believers? If you are not yet a believer, what should your response be to persecution against believers?

Fortunately, whether we are believers or non-believers, the Bible provides instructions for how to deal with persecution. Consider the following passages:

- Matthew 5:10-12: "Blessed are those who are persecuted because of righteousness, for theirs is the kingdom of heaven. Blessed are you when people insult you, persecute you and falsely say all kinds of evil against you because of me. Rejoice and be glad, because great is your reward in heaven, for in the same way they persecuted the prophets who were before you." (NIV)

- Matthew 5:43-48: "You have heard that it was said, 'Love your neighbor and hate your enemy.' But I tell you, love your enemies and pray for those who persecute you, that you may be children of your Father in heaven. He causes his sun to rise on the evil and the good, and sends rain on the righteous and the unrighteous. If you love those who love you, what reward will you get? Are not even the tax collectors doing that? And if you greet only your own people, what are you doing more than others? Do not even pagans do that? Be perfect, therefore, as your heavenly Father is perfect." (NIV)

- Acts 4:41-42: "The apostles left the Sanhedrin, rejoicing because they had been counted worthy of suffering disgrace for the Name. Day after day, in the temple courts and from house to house, they never stopped teaching and proclaiming the good news that Jesus is the Messiah." (NIV)

Most of us, even unbelievers, have heard Jesus's words about loving those who hate us, and perhaps even the passage where we are advised to bless those who persecute us. These are generally regarded as two of the most difficult commands of Jesus. But what of the last passage, where the apostles left the Sanhedrin rejoicing after they had been persecuted?

We believe this was written not only as a record of history, but with the purpose of encouraging early believers of how to act when they were persecuted. This was probably an example of "when", not "if". Followers of Christ in the first century were certainly going to suffer some form of persecution during their lifetime.

Back to the modern day. Does this passage also have application for us today? The answer is an uncompromising "Yes!" When we are persecuted, we must remember that there is a bigger plan at work and the persecution is a part of that plan. We pray that no one reading this book experiences physical persecution. But what of persecution at the office? What if you are escorted outside of your office building because you decide not to promote behavior that is contrary to the Scripture? What if you lose friends because you don't agree with their modern-day, anti-theistic beliefs? What if you are attacked on social media because you don't agree with the "morality of the day"? How should you respond?

While your specific situation will be intensely personal and likely nothing that we have gone through, the passages above seems pretty clear. Trust that there is a plan behind your persecution. Follow the plan, praying for God to work through it and bring more people into His kingdom.

Roger's Ramblings - How to Suffer

This is a tricky one: The world is full of suffering and there are many, many other people who are suffering much greater than I have, am currently suffering, or ever will suffer. Yes, my life has had it's ups and downs, but I am so blessed. I am presently writing this on a laptop in a city park after riding on my bicycle on the Legacy Trail. At no point was I ever concerned about bombs exploding around me. At no point was I ever concerned about being arrested for my faith.

I have been blessed to travel the world and have been in areas where people indeed are suffering on a continual basis. The rampant poverty in Rio de Janeiro, Brazil, results in suffering of all the people that live in the favelas. The same is true for citizens of Mexico, Thailand, Vietnam, and many other countries. Trips to China were great, but there was widespread suffering amongst the population against a strict government. As I am writing this section, war has blown up once again in the Middle East. People on both sides are suffering. As a result of satan and the fall of man, suffering will always be with us.

But, is there a way in which we can respond to suffering that becomes a blessing to others? I believe there is a way; actually, there are many ways.

In my previous books, I wrote about how to thrive whilst suffering through grave medical issues. The books were primarily focused on how my father endeavored to reach out to others and improve their lives while he was dealing with several types of cancer. The answer wasn't surprising: when we are suffering, we need to focus on others.

Dad was in constant pain as he fought prostate, skin, and then bladder cancer. But despite the pain, he made an effort to reach out to friends, neighbors, and acquaintances that were going through a hard time. When his cancer hurt so bad that he wasn't able to sleep at night, he still went and volunteered at a homeless shelter the next morning, a church committee meeting the next night, or phoned someone that he had recently learned was dealing with the same type of cancer he had fought. Would it have been easier to sit in his recliner and watch TV? Absolutely. But it wouldn't have made him feel any better.

One more example: good friends of mine went through a tragedy a few years ago. Did they respond by retreating to their house, never to make contact with others ever again? No, they continued with all of the opportunities where they were able to serve others. They even reached out to others going through a similar experience. They have truly been a blessing to others. Is the pain and suffering gone? Absolutely not. But by reaching out to others, they have been able to focus on something other than their own suffering.

Are you suffering today? How can you reach out to others?

(Shameless plug: If you are interested in learning more about the above books, check out my website: www.blauwshackmedia.com)

The Duality of Suffering

(Author's Note: The following is a message of inspiration that was written by the family mentioned in the preceding paragraph. Thank you Steve and Carla for your example of reminding us that suffering produces hope).

This isn't a sunshine and rainbows kind of message. Problems are going to come and with them, pain. You can choose whether problems and pain will make you bitter or make you better. God wants to turn pain into purpose!

I first delivered those words to a youth group on June 12, 2022. Why was that date significant? Because it was exactly two years to the day of our worst day in mine, my wife's, and family's life. At 2:30 in the afternoon, on a normal Friday, I was at the feet of our 15-year-old son's convulsing body as paramedics worked on him. How could something like this have happened?

I grew up in the church and knew conceptually that bad things happen because we live in a fallen world. But tragedies? To Christians? I mean, my dad was a pastor, I grew up going to church (Mom actually had me memorizing Scripture verses when I was 3 years old), I went to a Christian college where I was a ministry director and led accountability groups. I was a faithful employee, serving my customers for 27 years. I was faithful to my wife, a present and attentive father, even helping my kids memorize those same verses I memorized all those years! I was dedicated to my local church where I was an elder, led youth groups, and had been on several mission trips where I prayed for people and saw miracles happen. Throughout my life, I had worked diligently to live a life that would find favor with God and with men. Tragedies were supposed to happen to other people.

How was my Christian heritage helping now? What were those memorized verses doing for me now? Turns out, those verses helped out a lot because they reminded me of all the promises of God:

- *"And we know that in all things God works for the good of those who love him, who have been called according to his purpose." (Romans 8:28, NIV)*
- *"Come to me, all you who are weary and burdened, and I will give you rest." (Matthew 11:28, NIV)*
- *"Ask and it will be given to you; seek and you will find; knock and the door will be opened to you." (Matthew 7:7, NIV)*
- *"I have told you these things, so that in me you may have peace. In this world you will have trouble. But take heart! I have overcome the world." (John 16:33, NIV)*
- *"Dear friends, do not be surprised at the fiery ordeal that has come on you to test you, as though something strange were happening to you." (1 Peter 4:12, NIV)*
- *"Consider it pure joy, my brothers and sisters, whenever you face trials of many kinds, because you know that the testing of your faith produces perseverance." (James 1:2-3, NIV)*

Are we promised a bed of roses when we give our lives to Jesus, become Christians, and enter into the family of God? Of course not. We are still living in a fallen world. Read those two last verses above. Notice that the word "WHEN" is used instead of the word "IF"? So, what do we do with those promises? We don't like those. We want all the good promises, and none of the bad, don't we? If you haven't faced any significant trials, you haven't lived long enough.

Can a crisis be good? Can trials be good? Is there such a thing as a Good Crisis? How can we even call it a good crisis or a good trial? This seems to be an oxymoron, such as jumbo shrimp, freezer burn, icy hot, poor health, random order, seriously funny, working vacation, unbiased opinion, theoretical experience, same difference, static flow, etc. Good Crisis??

Thinking back to that Friday afternoon: What good was my faith now with a dying son on the afternoon of June 12th? Most would have had no clue because I hid it, that I was in quiet despair. I lost my confidence: as a dad, as a husband, as an employee, as an elder at my church, I thought I was going crazy - I was giving in to self-pity. I didn't want to die, but I didn't want to go on living any more. I had trouble praying; I had trouble reading the Bible. I took the family to church, but I really wasn't there. Random thoughts would enter my mind, like swerving onto the oncoming lane of traffic, making it look like an accident. My mind was bombarded with thoughts like: "You lost your son to suicide, how can God use you now?" "You'll never recover from this!" "This will mark you in shame forever." "You will be known for this the rest of your life." "God is through with you." "You're done." "There's no hope." I was giving in to all kinds of lies and negative self-talk.

You see, these were all lies. All my thoughts were selfish, how do I get through losing my first-born son? I was so wrecked in self-pity that I had trouble considering the impact of that loss on others: my wife (his mother), my children (his brothers and sisters), relatives, friends, acquaintances, etc.

The enemy uses lies; those are his only weapons. Pain, troubles, crises in life come, and the enemy will try to use the pains of life to get you to blame God or blame yourself to get you to destroy yourself. If that doesn't work, he will at least try to distract you or get you to numb the pain by self-medicating, by being consumed of yourself, thus being ineffective in this life. The devil has been twisting God's Word since the beginning of time and getting people messed up in the head.

How do you win in the Christian life? By getting up and trusting God to carry you. How do you overcome? By not giving up on God. How do you continue? -By never stopping/by never giving up on your faith and by focusing *on his truth. What do you do when problems come? You get up and keep running/ keep believing.*

We have it all wrong. James 4:7 tells us to, "Submit yourselves, then, to God. Resist the devil, and he will flee from you." (NIV) We have it backwards a lot of times: We resist God, submit to the devil, and give him license to stick around and torment us with lies. We need to take captive every thought and give it over to God if it doesn't line up with His Word.

Two years ago, to the day and I can talk about it and give praise and glory to God for getting us through! What the enemy meant for evil, God uses for good...if you let Him. Here are some things I've learned...

1. GOD WAS THERE

Pain will either make us bitter or better. God was with me when i found my son. God was weeping for my son at the same time I was. God knows what it is like to lose a son. He doesn't waste our tears; He uses them for His glory. God doesn't waste our pain; He uses it to bring good out of it if we let Him. The pain of crisis causes some to break, causes others to break records.

- *"If God hadn't been there for me, I never would have made it. The minute I said, 'I'm slipping, I'm falling,' your love, God, took hold and held me fast. When I was upset and beside myself, you calmed me down and cheered me up." (See Psalm 94:18-19, The Message)*
- *"God is our refuge and strength, an ever-present help in trouble." (Psalm 46:1, NIV)*
- *"The Lord is close to the brokenhearted and saves those who are crushed in spirit." (Psalm 34:18, NIV). Another translation records those words as, "If your heart is broken, you'll find God right there; if you're kicked in the gut, he'll help you catch your breath." (Psalm 34:18, The Message)*

2. HEALING OCCURS OVER TIME

Are we just meant to live in a mean and nasty place, and struggle and hold on for dear life until we finally make it to heaven some day? Survive to the bitter end or survive to the better end? Paul provides instructions to the believers in Rome that is relevant to us when we go through tragedies:

"Who shall separate us from the love of Christ? Shall trouble or hardship or persecution or famine or nakedness or danger or sword? As it is written: 'For your

sake we face death all day long; we are considered as sheep to be slaughtered.' No, in all these things we are more than conquerors through him who loved us. For I am convinced that neither death nor life, neither angels nor demons, neither the present nor the future, nor any powers, neither height nor depth, nor anything else in all creation, will be able to separate us from the love of God that is in Christ Jesus our Lord." (Romans 8:35-39, NIV)

Does it mean God no longer loves us if we have trouble or calamity, or are persecuted, or hungry, or destitute, or in danger, or threatened with death? No, DESPITE all these things, overwhelming victory is ours through Christ, who loved us. We need to claim the promise that in ALL these things we are more than conquerors through Him that loved us.

We even find encouragement in an old testament prophesy that Jesus was sent "to bind up the brokenhearted, to proclaim freedom for the captives and release from darkness for the prisoners, to comfort all who mourn, and provide for those who grieve—to bestow on them a crown of beauty instead of ashes, the oil of joy instead of mourning, and a garment of praise instead of a spirit of despair. Instead of your shame you will receive a double portion in your land, and instead of disgrace you will rejoice in your inheritance and everlasting joy will be yours." (promises found in Isaiah 61:1-7, NIV)

3. KEEP RUNNING WHEN PROBLEMS/CRISES COME

Any athlete knows that there will come a time during the event when the physical body and mental- self conspire together to promote the advantages of quitting. "Just stop and all the pain will go away", is their message. Only by pushing through these inner voices and feelings are athletes able to complete the race. The same is true for you and I when we go through problems, crises, and tragedies. We must keep moving forward. Consider the learnings from the following passages:

- 2 Corinthians 4:8 - We are pressed on every side by troubles, but we are not crushed. We are perplexed, but not driven to despair.
- 2 Corinthians 4:9 - We are hunted down, but God never abandons us. We get knocked down, but we get up again and keep going.
- Philippians 3:13 - Brothers and sisters, I can't consider myself a winner yet. This is what I do: I don't look back, I lengthen my stride, and I run straight toward the goal to win the prize that God's heavenly call offers in Christ Jesus.

- *Hebrews 12:1-3 - Since we are surrounded by so many examples of faith, we must get rid of everything that slows us down, especially sin that distracts us. We must run the race that lies ahead of us and never give up. We must focus on Jesus, the source and goal of our faith. He saw the joy ahead of him, so he endured death on the cross and ignored the disgrace it brought him. Now he holds the honored position—the one next to God the Father on the heavenly throne. Think about Jesus, who endured opposition from sinners, so that you don't become tired and give up.*

4. THE DUALITY OF SUFFERING

Yes, June 12th will forever be a day or loss in our household. But. It is also a day of rejoicing. We rejoice that our son is receiving his eternal reward in heaven. We rejoice in his final sacrifice of his earthly body so that others received healing. The doctors told us that the lives of seven people were forever altered positively through his sacrifice. Our worst day became their best day.

We are reminded of this promise in the book of Romans which says, "And we know that in all things God works for the good of those who love him, who have been called according to his purpose." (Romans 8:28, NIV). Those words are so powerful and spoke to our family: "in all things God". He doesn't work somethings for the good of those who love Him. No, in ALL things. He orchestrates good things to come from disasters.

Which reminds me of another oxymoron: Good Friday. Was the crucifixion good? Did the long-term result good? Jesus's worst day became our best day! God doesn't waste our pain but will use it for His glory if we let Him. God watched a son suffer and die too. Pain in the short term can, and should, lead to long term glory.

Yes, He promises that we will have trials, but He also promises never to leave us or forsake us. Consider these verses:

- *Matthew 28:20 - "I am with you always even unto the end of the world." (NIV)*
- *Joshua 1:9 - "Be strong and courageous; do not be frightened or dismayed, for the Lord your God is with you wherever you go." (NIV)*
- *James 1:12 — "Blessed is the one who perseveres under trial because, having stood the test, that person will receive the crown of life that the Lord has promised to those who love him." (NIV)*

- *Deuteronomy 31:6,8 - "Be strong and bold; have no fear or dread, because it is the Lord your God who goes before you. He will be with you; he will not fail you or forsake you." (NIV)*
- *Hebrews 10:35-36 - "So do not throw away this confident trust in the Lord. Remember the great reward it brings you! Patient endurance is what you need now, so that you will continue to do God's will. Then you will receive all that he has promised." (NIV)*
- *Revelation 21:4 - "He will wipe every tear from their eyes. There won't be any more death. There won't be any grief, crying, or pain,..."(NIV)*

Life is not about problems, it's about what you climb over and focus on that gives you a hope and a future. Faith is a fight - a fight for focus. And it is the fight of your life! Is your past your focus or is the future with God your focus? Are you going to be defined in life by how bad things were that came against you, or how you God helped you get through them? Are you going to be defined in life by what took you down or by how God helped you overcome? Are you resisting God or are you trusting Him to get you through anything? You have two choices: Submit to God and get help from a God who loves you or go it alone and hope for the best.

I will leave you with four more of the many promises found in the Bible:

- *1 Peter 5:6-10 - "Humble yourselves, therefore, under God's mighty hand, that he may lift you up in due time. Cast all your anxiety on him because he cares for you. Be alert and of sober mind. Your enemy the devil prowls around like a roaring lion looking for someone to devour. Resist him, standing firm in the faith, because you know that the family of believers throughout the world is undergoing the same kind of sufferings. And the God of all grace, who called you to his eternal glory in Christ, after you have suffered a little while, will himself restore you and make you strong, firm and steadfast." (NIV)*
- *Philippians 4:13 - "I can do all this through him who gives me strength." (NIV) - We can even make it through a death, even the death of a loved one.*
- *Isaiah 40:31 - "but those who hope in the Lord will renew their strength. They will soar on wings like eagles; they will run and not grow weary, they will walk and not be faint." (NIV)*
- *Isaiah 26:3 - "You will keep in perfect peace those whose minds are steadfast. because they trust in you." (NIV)*

May you always remember: A SETBACK is a SETUP for a COMEBACK!

JESUS IS: MY SAVIOR, MY DELIVERER, AND MY HOPE FOR THE FUTURE!

Do you know Jesus as your Savior, your Deliverer and your Hope for the future? What is stopping you from seeking Him today?

Written by Steve W.
   May, 2024

Reward

"Whoever has ears, let them hear what the Spirit says to the churches. The one who is victorious will not be hurt at all by the second death." (Revelation 2:11, NIV)

After identifying the problem and giving those words of warning, Jesus then pivots and provides words of encouragement to the believers in Smyrna. Notice that Jesus didn't promise relief from the suffering, or even from the pain of death itself. No, He promised them something greater. If the believers were able to endure the suffering, their victory would be found in the reward of eternal life. Talk about an awesome reward!

Do you want an awesome reward today? Stand firm during suffering for your reward in glory awaits. There is a song by Jimi Cravity called "Believe" that spoke to us after Dad passed away and is relevant to this topic. The lyrics speak to what a glorious sight it will be when we see each other in heaven as there will be no more suffering. How glorious it will be when we see Dad in heaven, dancing because there is no more bladder pain, loss of vision in his right eye, a gimpy foot, etc.

How about you? Will you be victorious through your suffering? Are you looking forward to the reward?

Points to Ponder with Jeff: Dealing with Suffering and Troubles

Let me give some points of application for our lives today. Sure, we don't live in Smyrna, but things have not changed that much.

You are Not Alone - Jesus understands (Verses 9-10)

The Christians in Smyrna were going through some hard times. We may not be facing the same things but all of us understand what hard times are. Jesus assures us He's got this. Not being afraid is not always easy. Jesus began His message by saying, "I was dead and now I am alive, forever and ever." He understood the hard times and ended up victorious. It is an interesting perspective.

Max Doner, in his book, "Revelation: A Manual of Spiritual Warfare" (p. 203) provides an illustration that puts our suffering into perspective, one that I had never thought of before. When we are threatened with suffering, it is akin to someone threatening to destroy a possession of ours that can be repurchased or regrown. Such a threat doesn't have great impact because the item in question can be replaced. Jesus was communicating to the believers in Smyrna (and to us) that their suffering shouldn't have great impact because they would be with Him in heaven forever.

That may be oversimplifying things but it is a heavenly perspective of the things we face here on this earth. Ephesians 2:6 promises that we are seated with Him in heavenly places so we can gain that perspective.

Jesus says in John 11:25, "I am the resurrection and the life. He that believes in Me, though he were dead, yet shall he live." (NIV)

He goes on to explain it more.

Suffering Won't Last Forever (Verse 10)

The phrase "Don't be afraid" is one of those things that is easier said than done, especially when it doesn't promise a bed of roses. He says you will suffer some things.

That brings up an interesting question: Why does God allow persecution and suffering for faith? Wouldn't it be much better if we didn't have to experience fear or pain or suffering? Yes. But that is what the promise of heaven is all about, not necessarily the promise of life here on this earth.

There is something that comes from the things here on this earth though: many times when we work through the tough times our faith is made stronger.

This verse ends with an interesting phrase – "You will suffer for ten days." This is an example of the use of numbers to represent a larger message, which again, is used many times in prophetic writings in the Bible. Suffering in this life may be a part of living in a world opposed to Jesus but it won't last forever. The phrase "10 days" can represent a period of time, not just 10 literal days. Jesus is saying that your time of suffering on this earth is not eternal. It will be a time of testing. There will be suffering but it is all temporary compared to the eternity of heaven.

So what is the outcome of the hard times?

There is a crown of life Waiting for You (Verse 10)

You may have heard of a man named Polycarp. He lived in Smyrna and some 60 years after John wrote Revelation he was burned at the stake by the Roman government for his faith. He was one of the first well-known Christian martyrs. We know that Polycarp was killed in 155 AD when he was 86 years old. It is feasible that he was alive as a young man in his early 20's in the church at Smyrna and heard the words of John read to him. If so, they must have made an impact on him because he was given the opportunity several times to renounce his faith in front of a large audience. He never relented and was killed for his faith.

Jesus's words of "But if you remain faithful even when facing death, I will give you the crown of life. . . Whoever is victorious will not be harmed by the second death." were true for the people of Smyrna, they were true for Polycarp and they are true for us today. Jesus is telling us to see beyond what we face in this world and what is waiting for us in heaven.

Jesus is telling us to remain faithful, even in the worst of circumstances because He has gone before us to prepare a place for us. A place that He describes at the end of the book of Revelation as a place with no more suffering, no more pain, no more crying. There is a reward waiting for us if we can be faithful, even when facing death.

Let me leave you with the challenge that Jesus gives to the people at Smyrna:

Are you willing to make the effort and do what it takes? (Verse 11)

Are you willing to listen? Are you willing to listen to the Spirit? Are you willing to do work to understand what He is saying? Are you willing to assimilate what He is saying into your life? Understand, there is a difference between hearing and listening. Hearing means you hear noise. Listening means you transform the noise you hear into words that change your life.

Do you remember what the theme is that we are using for Revelation? Right – We win! That's what Jesus wants for us. He wants us to Win!

Pergamum

Background of Pergamum

This letter is addressed to the Christians who lived in the city of Pergamum. In John's day it had a population of about 180,000. All of the cities that are addressed in Revelation were Roman cities that had the pagan religions of the day that created conflicts for followers of Jesus. However, Pergamum, an architectural and cultural center, was considered the worst of them all.

Pergamum's history also points to the idea of worshiping the king as a god even before Rome came along and demanded it. Pergamum was considered a very religious city but not in a good sense. The practice of emperor worship was celebrated on Pergamum's coinage in this period. Local rulers had been worshiped before the Roman period, and Pergamum was one of the first cities of Asia to build a temple to a Roman emperor, making it a center of the cult.

It was also considered the home of the god Zeus – chief of the Greek and Roman gods. There was a temple built to Zeus there in the city. Some say that when approached from a distance it looked like a huge throne – imagery which plays into the words of Jesus when He says "where satan has his throne"

They also had another god they worshiped – the god Asclepius, the serpent god. This god, to Christians, was the very image of satan as depicted in the garden of Eden. So, when Jesus says, "I know where you live – where satan has his throne" it would have really connected with the people because of the foreign and false gods they saw around them.

In Case You Forgot, Jesus is the Author of the Letter

"To the angel of the church in Pergamum write: These are the words of him who has the sharp, double-edged sword." (Revelation 2:12, NIV)

We're going to need you to put your thinking hats on for a little while. In ancient times, guns and other projectile-based weapons did not exist. Weapons were basically designed for up-close-and-personal fighting (except for the bow and arrow, but that's a whole different story so we will put that weapon on the back burner). Think back to the fighting scenes in movies such as Gladiator, Ben-Hur, Robin Hood, Chariots of Fire...nope, not that last one. But you get the idea: when nations or groups decided to fight other groups or nations, it was predominately done with edged weapons such as knives or swords. We won't bore you with the details, but in fighting with edged weapons, your ability to incur damage on the person trying to kill you is significantly diminished if your sword only has one bladed edge. Advantage: Your opponent. If you were conscripted to fight, you wanted a double-edged sword to maximize your potential to make it back home to your family.

John's letter reminds us that not only is Jesus the author of the letter, He is a mighty warrior. Let's skip forward a little bit in the text so that we can understand why that particular description of Jesus was relevant to the believers in Pergamum. As mentioned earlier, the city of Pergamum was not a pleasant place to live in, and even worse for people who, by their religion, chose not to participate in the immorality that was prevalent. To say that those believers were oppressed on all sides by friends, neighbors, and acquaintances probably is not an exaggeration.

Now put yourself in the place of those believers. Everyone is against you. But yet, you still choose to stay true to the faith that everyone in the city despises. So they hate you even more and the oppression gets greater. Reading a letter where Jesus is described as a mighty warrior would probably give you some comfort, right? Knowing that God is on your side is going to help you sleep better at night. A study of the complete scriptures indicates that the interpretation of the double-edged sword is the Word of God by which God created the heavens and the earth. That's power right there!

We enjoy using Hollywood and our entertainment culture to help explain Biblical concepts. There is just something refreshing about using what they meant for entertainment to help further the Kingdom. For this point, we are reminded of a war movie that came out recently called Devotion. The movie itself had a great message, but there was one scene that demonstrated the importance of knowing that great power backed you up. The movie was set during the Korean War and one of the scenes focused on the battle at the Chosin Reservoir. This battle was particularly difficult for the American forces to make headway against the enemy, and in fact, they were getting beaten pretty handily. The American troops were dejected and resigned to the fate that they were going to die. Until the planes piloted by the major characters flew over the American line and started shooting at the enemy. In the film, the Americans are portrayed as cheering when the planes flew over the lines. The troops were cheering because they realized that the planes brought tremendous power to their side of the fight.

Think back to the believers at Pergamum. Do you think that it was a coincidence that Jesus had John proclaim His mightiness?

Let's get back to the title and purpose of this book. Is there anything in your life right now where you could use a mighty warrior on your side? He's right there waiting for you to ask.

Good Job

"I know where you live—where Satan has his throne. Yet you remain true to my name. You did not renounce your faith in me, not even in the days of Antipas, my faithful witness, who was put to death in your city—where Satan lives." (Revelation 2:13, NIV)

Basically, the message to the believers in Pergamum is: "You live in a cesspool but you've stayed faithful. Great job team! Against all odds, which are considerable, you've managed to stay true to your faith!"

Jesus commends those who stand firm in their faith. He says the Christians in Pergamum did not renounce Him, even though one of their fellow Christians, Antipas, was put to death for his faith.

According to Christian tradition, John the Apostle ordained Antipas as bishop of Pergamum during the reign of the Roman emperor Nero. The traditional accounts go on to say Antipas was martyred during either the reign of Nero or Domitian, by being burned in a brazen bull-shaped altar the Romans used for casting out demons worshiped by the local population.

For them to see this happen to their leader and not renounce their faith says a lot about them. If you saw one of your friends put to death for their faith that would make you think a little. Jesus lets them know that He has seen their faithfulness.

But....

"Nevertheless, I have a few things against you: There are some among you who hold to the teaching of Balaam, who taught Balak to entice the Israelites to sin so that they ate food sacrificed to idols and committed sexual immorality. Likewise, you also have those who hold to the teaching of the Nicolaitans." (Revelation 2:14-15, NIV)

As with all the other churches, things are not all sunshine and butterflies for the believers in Pergamum. There are people within their faith community that are not right with God.

But first, we need to give a little of the back story here for this to make sense. Jesus is referring to something that happened in the Old Testament in the book of Numbers, chapters 22-25. When the Children of Israel were wandering around in the wilderness for 40 years they entered into the land of Moab. Balak was the king of Moab and saw how many Israelites there were and knew that he could not defeat them. He contacted a man name Balaam, who was reported to be a prophet of God and offered him money to come and curse the children of Israel. Balaam went and tried but God would only let him give a blessing to the children of Israel. Balaam really wanted the money though, so he told king Balak, "I can't curse them but I know how to bring God's wrath against them. Just send some women (who were probably temple prostitutes) into the Israelite camp and let them infiltrate and cause the men to partake in the temple prostitution and participate in BAAL worship." His plan worked and soon Baal worship entered into the children of Israel and they came under the wrath of God.

Apparently there were some in the church of Pergamum that were okay with the false teaching going on concerning their morality and the moral teachings of what was right and wrong. They would be the ones considered holding on to the teaching of Balaam – practice of immorality.

There was also group called the Nicolaitans who basically taught the same concept – that sexual immorality was okay. Their reasoning was that sexual immorality only impacted the physical and not the spiritual. None of this was healthy and Jesus knew where it would lead if it wasn't dealt with quickly.

Of all the letters to the seven churches, the letter to Pergamum likely has the most relevance to living in our society. But hoo-boy, talk about the political and societal hot potatoes that would result from a conversation about sexual morality in this book. So we're going to skip it because it really isn't conducive to this passage of scripture.

The important aspect of this portion of the letter is found in the next section because, as we learned earlier, if you're sinning, then you need to.....

Repent!

"Repent therefore! Otherwise, I will soon come to you and will fight against them with the sword of my mouth." (Revelation 2:16, NIV)

There's that word again: Repent. It must be stated again: This is such a powerful word in Christianity. The saving grace of the Gospel of Jesus is that sinners can become whole again, providing that they repent of their sins. This is encouraging to us today and must have been encouraging to the believers that had gone astray in Pergamum. Of course there is no way to know the numbers of believers that actually did repent after reading John's letter, but one can hope that it was a large number.

It's interesting that the believers in Pergamum were given a different "If this, then that" clause than the believers in Ephesus. If you recall, the believers in Ephesus were told if they didn't repent, then Jesus would remove their lampstand, which was their chance at eternal life. The believers in Pergamum were told that if they didn't repent, then Jesus would actually fight against them with the sword of his mouth. It would appear that the "them" in this text is the believers in Pergamum that had drifted away from the faith and were more aligned with society and culture. We can't speak for you, but the prospect of fighting against Jesus would scare us back to the straight and narrow path of life.

That is a pretty compelling argument for the need to abandon immorality and get back to a life of faith in Jesus. No one wants to fight against Jesus; it would be pointless because it would be over in a millisecond. A comparison would be the old video clip of Bambi vs Godzilla. Picture a serene setting with a peaceful deer and then, Wham! A foot flattens the deer. That's like humans going against Jesus. Except that it would be over much quicker.

So repent. Why? Because of the second part of the "If this, then that" clause. If you repent, then the reward is yours. And what have we learned thus far about the reward?

Rewards

"Whoever has ears, let them hear what the Spirit says to the churches. To the one who is victorious, I will give some of the hidden manna. I will also give that person a white stone with a new name written on it, known only to the one who receives it." (Revelation 2:17, NIV)

(Jeff does a fantastic job in the next section describing the reward. His explanation provides a clear picture, based upon a solid scriptural foundation, of the reward waiting those in Pergamum that repented. So we won't take any of his thunder in this section. Spoiler alert: It's heaven.)

Points to Ponder with Jeff: What Jesus Knows / What We Need to Know

I want to emphasize the importance and influence of the local church. The local church plays a role in God's big picture for His kingdom. The kingdom of God on earth is only as strong as the local church. In chapters two and three we see how intimately Jesus sees and understands the local church. He speaks to each church individually and addresses their unique qualities and shortcomings. We will see an example of both as we look at the church of Pergamum.

I want to walk through the letter to Pergamum by making application and sharing relevant background information at the same time. Remember, Revelation is a message not only to the first century church, but also to us today. Here are some things I think Jesus wants us to learn today:

First, Jesus understands the world in which we are living:

Just like the other two letters to the churches we have looked at, Ephesus and Smyrna, Jesus identifies Himself to the church of Pergamum. He uses the images that were presented of Him in Chapter 1:16 – the one who "has the sharp, double-edged sword". This imagery is found also in Rev 19 when Jesus comes as conqueror riding a white horse - "I saw heaven standing open and there before me was a white horse, whose rider is called Faithful and True. . . Out of his mouth comes a sharp sword with which to strike down the nations." (Revelation 19:11-15, NIV). Jesus delivers His message to the church with all authority and power. In the next phrase (verse 13) we find that His power goes beyond just an image of strength to one of divinity – all knowing.

Just as Jesus knew Pergamum, He knows where you live. He knows the church you attend. If you don't attend a local church, He knows them all. We don't have any temples to Zeus or Asclepius but do we have things that people put before God? Sure there are: recreation, sports, entertainment, wealth – just to name a few. You can fill in the rest of the blanks. If He knows what is here around us He also knows what can get in our way of living fully for Him. That is a simple but important thing to remember.

From this point of application, Jesus transitions and goes on to share some very specific things that He knows about the world in which the believers in Pergamum lived.

Second, Jesus knows what we do – vs. 13b - 14a

Jesus complimented the believers in Pergamum for staying true to His name, even in spite of extremely challenging circumstances, but He goes on to be honest with them saying He has seen their faith but He does have a few things against them. Why would He go on to say that? Haven't they done enough? He goes on to say that because He knows what He sees will harm them if they let it go if they ignore it. It is not with eyes of condemnation He sees them: it is with eyes of love.

It is good for us to realize that Jesus does know what we do and what can be an issue for us. Every believer should live life with a sense of accountability to God. We don't like that word because it means that we have to submit to someone else's knowledge. It means we might have to admit that we don't always have life figured out and that we don't always do what we should have done. But again, we need to understand that Jesus looks at us not with eyes of condemnation, but with eyes of love. He doesn't want us to do harm to ourselves. He wants us to know what to avoid.

Thirdly, avoid compromising on what is "right and wrong" (verses 14-16):

Today the behavior described in verses 14-16 would be expressed like this, "I can do whatever I want as long as it doesn't hurt anyone else. I set my own moral code."

With that as background, what do you think Jesus would have to say to our culture today? In what direction do we seem to be heading today? I don't think it would surprise anyone if I said that morals in America today are going down the toilet. What is "right" should be determined by the Bible but that is not the norm used in our present society.

From a 2016 Barna Research Report "Three-quarters (74%) of Millennials (those between 27 – 42 years old) agree strongly or somewhat with the statement, "Whatever is right for your life or works best for you is the only truth you can know," compared to only 38 percent of Elders (those born before 1946). The same study showed Two-thirds of American adults either believe moral truth is relative to circumstances (44%) or have not given it much thought (21%). (The End of Absolutes: America's New Moral Code, Research Releases in Culture & Media – May 25, 2016)

So, what is Jesus's final word to Pergamum and us? It may surprise you.

Finally, He promises us amazing blessings (verse 17):

Jesus again closes the letter by saying, "Listen to what I have to say and take it to heart." Hang in there. Remain faithful – even when it is tough. If you overcome there are some amazing promises for you. Jesus promises "the hidden Manna" – Manna in the Old Testament was food that which gave life in the desert, yet it was temporary, it had to be replenished everyday. Jesus takes that and applies it to life eternal. What is the hidden manna? It is what Jesus has to offer that the people in His day (and today) have a hard time finding and seeing – He is the "bread of life".

In the book of John, Jesus says, "I am the bread of life. Your forefathers ate the manna in the desert, yet they died. But here is the bread that comes down from heaven, which a man may eat and not die. I am the living bread that came down from heaven. If anyone eats of this bread, he will live forever." (John 6:48-51, NIV) He says that He is the manna that comes down from heaven. It is Jesus that gives life, life eternal.

Jesus then promises a "white stone". It stands for forgiveness and being set free, innocent before God. Have you ever been in a courtroom or at least seen a trial on TV? What is everyone waiting for? The verdict. In the Roman court system in the days of Revelation, when people were taken to court and charged of a crime a *judge or panel of judges would make the decision. They had a simple way of handing down a verdict. They would cast a black stone or they would cast a white stone. The black stone meant guilty. The white stone meant innocent.*

What does Jesus promise? A white stone to those that overcome. Your innocence was made possible because Jesus paid the price for your sin on the cross. I don't know about you, but I want a white stone with my name written on it.

Thyatira

Background on Thyatira

This is the longest of the letters to the seven churches, yet it is addressed to the least known, least important and least remarkable of the cities. But it still was an important church to Jesus. The place where the ancient city stood is now the site of the modern day city of Akhisar and very few archaeological digs have been done there.

Here the challenge or threat against Christians was not like the other churches where the Roman government was persecuting the Christians; it was more of a social, cultural, and economic threat that came from the industry of the city. Thyatira was known as a city full of tradesmen and trade guilds or unions. It produced wool, linen, garments, pottery, metal working, the dying of cloth and many other trades. This is affirmed in Acts 16 where Thyatira is mentioned because a woman named Lydia, who was a seller of purple was from there. She became a Christian after hearing Paul share about Christ.

Thyatira was what we would call more of a "blue collar" town full of workers and tradesmen. There is a town that fit this characterization in Central Illinois. The town of Decatur, IL used to be a town of big industry companies like Staley, ADM, Caterpillar, and Firestone Tire. It was also a very strong union town. If someone tried to build something without using the local unions, you were likely to incur the wrath of the unions.

In Thyatira each guild union had its own particular god that they paid homage to, having festivals and feasts on a regular basis in the hopes of pleasing their god so that their industry would flourish. This became a problem for Christians who were to worship only one God and abstain from sexual immorality, which most of these pagan worship practices included. If the Christian quit the trade guild, he lost his ability to buy and sell in the economic activity of his trade. That had implications for something later referred to in Revelation as the "mark of the beast", 666.

Pay Attention to This Letter!

"To the angel of the church in Thyatira write: These are the words of the Son of God, whose eyes are like blazing fire and whose feet are like burnished bronze." (Revelation 2:18, NIV)

Hopefully at this point in the book, our position on the enlightenment of man is that we are all fallen creatures: everyone has sinned at least once in their lives and no one is perfect. As a result of this, no matter how friendly we are with people or how much we love those closest to us, from time to time strife enters into relationships. It's entirely unavoidable; we are going to make people mad at us and we will be upset with other people.

Think back to one of those instances where you made someone mad. Perhaps it was a parent, a spouse, a close friend, or perhaps even a customer. There were physical clues that the other person was upset with you prior to a change in language or a terse discussion. Many times, the anger is manifest through the eyes through a piercing gaze, a furrowed brow, or a change in the proportion of pupil to the rest of the eye. Sometimes, this is all it takes to begin conflict resolution because it lets the other person know that there is a problem that needs to be solved, immediately. When we were children, we all knew when our parents were upset with us because they gave us "the face" or the "stink eye."

Pretend, now that you are the leader of the church in Thyatira (remember, we've stated that the "angel of the church in Thyatira" is a leader in the church). A letter from John, a greatly respected leader in the church, arrives to your attention. You eagerly unroll the paper and begin reading the letter, expecting to read words of praise and encouragement from John. And the first words you read describe Jesus as having "eyes like blazing fire". Your heart drops; this letter is not going to be filled with images of sunshine and butterflies.

Sometimes we need strong words to get us to focus. This letter was important and the leader needed to take the words seriously. As you will discover in the following sections, the Thyatira church needed what we would today call a "course correction".

Good Job

"I know your deeds, your love and faith, your service and perseverance, and that you are now doing more than you did at first." (Revelation 2:19, NIV)

After getting the reader's attention, Jesus reverts back to the method of praising some aspect of the church. He is pleased with some key things that have been happening in Thyatira – they are putting their faith in action, "your deeds, love, faith, service, and perseverance". Then He says that not only have they accomplished those things but they are growing in them. Growth is the key, the standard we all should set for ourselves.

How many aspects of your life fall within this category of growth? We spoke earlier about the human tendency to become complacent and to rest on our laurels once we have become good at a hobby, a job, a sport, etc. It takes a different mindset to continue growth towards excellence. In fact, our society has made an industry of growing towards excellence; there are books, seminars, classes and many other resources that promise to teach us to adopt this mindset.

The believers in Thyatira understood this concept and seemed to be accomplishing the goal of making today better than yesterday. They were praised in all the key aspects of Christianity. Their deeds were improving. Their love to others was improving. Their faith was strengthening. Their service to their fellow man was improving. Their perseverance in a hostile culture was improving. On paper at least, it would seem that this church was growing stronger. But this facet of the church would quickly be challenged.

Compromising with Jezebel

"Nevertheless, I have this against you: You tolerate that woman Jezebel, who calls herself a prophet. By her teaching she misleads my servants into sexual immorality and the eating of food sacrificed to idols. I have given her time to repent of her immorality, but she is unwilling. So I will cast her on a bed of suffering, and I will make those who commit adultery with her suffer intensely, unless they repent of her ways. I will strike her children dead. Then all the churches will know that I am he who searches hearts and minds, and I will repay each of you according to your deeds." (Revelation 2:20-23, NIV)

None of us like to receive bad news. Who of us haven't put off opening that letter we receive in the mail that we are certain contains bad news such as an overdue bill, a bad medical diagnosis, a rejection letter from college, or a jury duty notice. Once we work up the courage to open the letter and read what it says, we want to seal the letter back up and claim ignorance. After all, if we didn't read the letter, what's to say that we actually received it? The letter probably got lost in the mail.

Possibly that's what went through the mind of the leader of the Thyatira church. He probably read it a few times to make sure that the message was actually intended for their community of believers. The issue stemmed from the tolerance that the believers afforded to a way of thinking that as long as your spiritual self believed in Jesus then you could do anything with your physical body because they were completely separate entities. Believers were convinced that they could abide by Jesus's teachings and commands in their mind while conforming to society's moral principles (or the lack thereof).

After mentally accepting that the letter was an accurate description of the church's compromise, there must have been a temptation to burn the letter as it was going to be difficult to deliver to the believers. Many of the believers would have been familiar with scriptures, knew about the teaching of Jezebel, and would have no problem applying it to their lives. But for us, perhaps some background on Jezebel is necessary.

Jezebel is first mentioned in the Old Testament book of 1 Kings: "Ahab son of Omri did more evil in the eyes of the Lord than any of those before him. He not only considered it trivial to commit the sins of Jeroboam son of Nebat, but he also married Jezebel daughter of Ethbaal king of the Sidonians, and began to serve Baal and worship him." (1 Kings 16:30-32, NIV) For context, Baal was a pagan god of fertility back in Old Testament times. Following Baal involved many practices of sexual immorality, which was contrary to the beliefs of the Jewish people. She doesn't sound too bad right now, right? Perhaps she was a fine outstanding young lady who was captured or required to marry Ahab. Perhaps, but not very probable.

King Ahab, described as doing "more evil in the eyes of the Lord than any of those before him", was not a decent fellow. He most likely looked for women with similar mentality. Worship of gods other than the true God of Israel seemed a prerequisite to be married to Ahab. We later learn that Jezebel was not a nice person at the beginning of chapter 18: "While Jezebel was killing off the Lord's prophets..." (1 Kings 18:4, NIV)

At some point, Ahab set his sights on battling Elijah, one of God's prophets. In 1 Kings 18 Elijah had a confrontation with Ahab and all the prophets of Baal & Asherah – 950 in all. The confrontation was a grown-up version of "My God is better than your gods", albeit with deadly consequences. God proved Himself to all the false prophets by sending down fire from heaven at the word of Elijah. This was done on a moment's notice in contrast to all the prophets of Baal who called for it all day from their gods and nothing happened. Needless to say, after the fireworks, Ahab had all his prophets put to death.

This did not please Jezebel, especially since she was the one to get her husband the king and a whole bunch of other Israelites to follow her gods. She went ballistic:

"Now Ahab told Jezebel everything Elijah had done and how he had killed all the prophets with the sword. So Jezebel sent a messenger to Elijah to say, 'May the gods deal with me, be it ever so severely, if by this time tomorrow I do not make your life like that of one of them.'" (1 Kings 19:1-2, NIV)

Grumpy, right?

What was Elijah's reaction? The third verse of 1 Kings 19 tells us that Elijah was afraid and ran for his life. This was the same man who stood up to the 950 prophets with no problem but did not dare to stand up against Jezebel. This is perhaps due to the fact that Jezebel was scary, everyone feared her. 1 Kings 21:25 gives a summary of Ahab and Jezebel: "There was never a man like Ahab, who sold himself to do evil in the eyes of the Lord, urged on by Jezebel his wife". (1 Kings 21:25, NIV) Have you ever heard of anyone today naming their daughter Jezebel? You probably will never find that name in those books that provide a list of baby names because that name came to represent all that was evil.

Jesus calls out that "woman Jezebel" in the church at Thyatira. They were doing in the church what the original Jezebel was doing in the OT – turning people away from God with her teaching. She claimed to be a prophetess – a teacher in the church. Jesus basically says to the church at Thyatira that God's judgment will be brought down on those who followed her teaching and her ways.

Was there actually a living person in the church that was named Jezebel? Probably not. Most likely it was a metaphor to the morality practices of Roman society. The letter was a reminder to the believers that they were to be separate from the Romans.

Roger's Ramblings: Tolerance vs Acceptance & Compromise

"Nevertheless, I have this against you: You tolerate that woman Jezebel, who calls herself a prophet." (Revelation 2:20, NIV)

Many translations of the Bible use the word "tolerate" in this verse as to how the believers were treating the teachings of Jezebel. The King James version actually uses a different word: "because thou sufferest that woman Jezebel" (Revelation 2:20, KJV). The Greek word is "Eao" and this is the only time that particular word is used in the New Testament. The definition of the original term is to "let be", "to permit", or "to leave alone." Thus, a rephrasing of the above verse would then be that the believers in Thyatira "let Jezebel and her contrary teachings be". Or that the believers in Thyatira "permit Jezebel and her contrary teachings to exist". Or that the believers in Thyatira "leave Jezebel and her contrary teachings alone."

Regardless of the specific translation, Jesus seems to have four issues in Thyatira. First, and foremost, that Jezebel was leading the people into practices that were in direct contradiction to His teachings. It goes without saying that He didn't approve of Jezebel. The second issue was that ordinary people were following Jezebel rather than His teachings. This ties directly into our admonition that Jesus doesn't want anyone to miss out on eternal life. Third, certain numbers of His followers were straying from His teachings and following the practices of Jezebel. This is directly tied to the fourth issue, which is that the believers stood by as people began to abandon their faith to those same evil practices and false teachings in increasing numbers.

See any relevance to our society today?

Earlier in the book, we discussed the society's approach to the word "tolerance" (see "Relevance to Our Society" section). We would be hard-pressed to argue that what our society views as tolerance is actually "acceptance". We must accept anything and everything, even if it is contrary to our upbringing, morals, and beliefs. Society attacks those who don't accept all of their practices and calls them intolerant, among other politically-charged words. People that are intolerant are now labeled as "haters". Society understands that once acceptance replaces tolerance, compromise is a small obstacle to overcome on the road to abandonment of morality.

At the beginning of this book, we promised to stay out of politics and we will honor that commitment in this section. Rather than attacking one political party or the other, we will throw every political party under the bus. Discussion about this slippery slope from tolerance to compromise is necessary because the comparisons between Thyatira and our society appear to be greater today than at other points in history.

When a person is accused of being intolerant, what is the real meaning behind that attack? In some instances the person being attacked is generally intolerant of a person whose beliefs are different. But I would argue that this is the minority of cases: often the attack is directed at people who are minding their own business, not disparaging those with different beliefs.

In the majority of cases, there is a "agree to disagree" mentality. This seems to line up with the definition of tolerance and falls in line with the conditions in Thyatira. But this is not sufficient for our society because it doesn't allow for the ultimate objection. When someone is labeled as intolerant, the unspoken definition that is being applied is one of "nonacceptance". We are being told that it is not enough to simply tolerate those with different beliefs as us; we must accept their beliefs as facts and reality.

The ultimate outcome of this mindset is that there is no such thing as truth. There is no such thing as Right or Wrong. Everyone's truth is reality and we must all accept this new reality. Is it any wonder that our culture is drifting further and further away from Biblical teaching, principles, and morality?

The letter to Thyatira teaches us, therefore, an important lesson. We simply cannot stand on the sidelines with a mindset of tolerance, a mindset of ignoring these contrary teachings.

What can we do? How to minimize these modern-day teachings of Jezebel in our churches and culture? We've been taught for many years that as Christians we are to "love the sinner but hate the sin". This philosophy has been long-lasting because it is rooted in Scripture: God loves us despite our sin.

But is this consistent with a tolerant mindset? If you steal my lunch out of the refrigerator at work one day, tolerance tells me to not respond to you in anger. Perhaps there is a reason why you are sinning in that particular manner. But what happens if you steal my lunch everyday? Tolerance will lead to acceptance by me *which will in turn lead me to comprise my belief that stealing is wrong. This is just an example. The principles remain any time we choose a sinful activity time and time and time again rather than work to eliminate that behavior - gossiping about a co-worker, cheating on your work expense report, cheating on a test at school, lying about a neighbor. The list goes on and on.*

At some point, there has to be accountability that you're simply not working to correct your behavior. At some point, we need to realize that the longer we tolerate sinful behavior, the more we become like the believers in Thyatira. I don't know about you, but I don't want to be "cast on a bed of suffering" or to "suffer intensely" with Jezebel.

I do like those next few words though, "unless they repent of her ways". (Revelation 2:22, NIV) Let's all strive to repent of all our sinful ways and strive to make tomorrow better than today.

You Have Two Options

"Now I say to the rest of you in Thyatira, to you who do not hold to her teaching and have not learned Satan's so-called deep secrets, 'I will not impose any other burden on you, except to hold on to what you have until I come.'" (Revelation 2:24-25, NIV)

The believers in Thyatira were presented with two options to bridge the gap between their practices before this letter, and the reward of eternal life. The two options are consistent with what we've read so far in John's letters but this is the first time that the options are used together for one group of believers. The first option was to repent, while the second option was to "keep on keeping on". Let's look at each option.

Option 1: Repent

In contrast to the language used with the previous churches, the call to repentance for the believers of Thyatira is a veiled option. After calling out Jezebel, Jesus goes on to say that He gave her the option to repent but she was "unwilling". He then goes on to say that those who follow her will suffer "intensely" but not if they repent. This message is consistent with our previous discussion about repentance: Jesus doesn't want anyone to miss out on Heaven and eternal life. This desire is so great that He was willing to let those both in the church and in society (followers of Jezebel) repent of their evil ways, and partake in the reward of eternal life.

The good news for us is that this desire of Jesus that everyone experience eternal life was strong for the believers in Thyatira and is strong for us today as well. His offer of repentance is open for all who have sinned.

Option 2: Keep on Keeping On

This option was intended specifically for those believers within the church that had chosen not to compromise their beliefs and correlates perfectly with our approach to society today. It wouldn't be easy, but the rewards of a life well-lived were tremendous: spending eternity with Jesus. If you choose not to conform and compromise your beliefs, life will not be easy. You could be bullied or alienated from friends and family members. You may even suffer persecution from standing for your beliefs. But take heart: God will be near as you stand firm. Not convinced? Check out the following verses:

- Exodus 14:13
- 2 Chronicles 20:17
- Psalm 20:8
- Psalm 33:11
- Proverbs 10:25
- Proverbs 12:7
- Matthew 10:22
- Matthew 24:13
- Mark 13:13
- Luke 21:19
- 1 Corinthians 15:58
- 1 Corinthians 16:13
- 2 Thessalonians 2:13-15
- James 5:8
- 1 Peter 5:9

There was, of course, a third option, which was for the believers to choose to wholly abandon their faith and conform to the world, in which case, their access to eternal life was eliminated. Unfortunately, a great number of believers chose option 3 because history tells us that the church in Thyatira largely disappeared in the second century. As a result of compromise, many people were unable to experience the rewards written about in verses 26-29.

Rewards

"To the one who is victorious and does my will to the end, I will give authority over the nations— that one 'will rule them with an iron scepter and will dash them to pieces like pottery'—just as I have received authority from my Father. I will also give that one the morning star. Whoever has ears, let them hear what the Spirit says to the churches." (Revelation 2:26-29, NIV)

To the over-comers, to the ones doing what God wants them to do, He gives two interesting promises. First, He will give them authority over the nations. Does that mean we will each get our own little kingdom to rule over? Get a castle with a moat to live in? Maybe, but more likely is that the imagery simply means that we will reign with Christ, sharing in His Kingdom. Hopefully by now you realize that the phrase, "His Kingdom", is another word for Heaven. This is the great reward promised to those from Thyatira who repent and/or stick to their beliefs amongst a society that is against them.

The second thing promised is "the morning star". This is also one of those symbolic passages where it is best to let scripture interpret scripture. The phrase "morning star" is used one other time in Revelation and its meaning is very clear. In Revelation 22:16, John writes, "I, Jesus, have sent my angel to give you this testimony for the churches. I am the Root and the Offspring of David, and the bright Morning Star." We believe Jesus is offering to the church at Thyatira, and to us, Himself. He is saying "I will be everything you need. I will be with you for eternity." Is there a greater reward?

Points to Ponder with Jeff: Hang On to the Things that Matter

Right now I want you to think about what it takes to win for a moment. My guess is that every one of you here at one time or another in your life did something that you wanted to win at. It may be something as small as a game. I tend to be a competitive person and like to win at anything I do. When our daughters were young and I would play games with them sometimes I would let them win - that was hard for me to do!

But I learned that some things are more important to winning the game of Chutes and Ladders or Pretty Pretty Princess. But there are things that do make a huge difference. John writes down the words he is given in the book of Revelation to encourage Christians everywhere, in many different situations, over many years. He wants us to win when it comes to eternal life.

As I studied the letter to the church I saw 5 things that stood out to me that are instructions that support the big picture message of the book of Revelation – that message being "We Win!" As we walk through Revelation 2:18-22 let's discover those 5 things. I believe there are certain things that you need to hold onto when you want to win.

Number 1: Don't forget who is in charge (Verse 18)

It is to the people of the church that Jesus addresses. He is introduced with the same imagery that He is described with in Rev 1:14,15: "eyes of blazing fire and feet of burnished bronze". Those are images that depict piercing authority and strength. He is one that will not back down from the challenges being brought to His children, His church.

We still need to remember today that Jesus is the one in charge. His strength and authority have not diminished over time. He still is Lord over the church and looks down upon His church. Don't ever lose sight of who He is. Hold on to the fact that He is still the one in charge.

Number 2: Build on your strengths (Verse 19)

Rather than talking about each one of those things I want us to think of how the strengths are all intertwined together. The believers were living in a world that opposed much of what they stood for and believed; so what were those non-Christians seeing when they observed the believers?

Who you are as a Christian is seen through your deeds, which come from your love, that is an outgrowth of your faith, which expresses itself in your service, and that is offered for the long haul. None of this should be a checklist to get brownie points with God, but rather, blend these things all together so that your life should be an expression of how others see Jesus in you. If we can keep these in balance and make them an expression of who we are, we are one step closer to winning.

Number 3: Don't close your eyes to what is going on around you (Verses 20-23)

Do the words of Jesus in this passage mean that God is a God of hate and not of love? No. It is His love that gives everyone the offer of forgiveness and salvation. That is what it means when He says in vs. 21 "I have given her time to repent of her immorality, but she is unwilling." God, as a holy and just God, cannot close His eyes to sin. He sees it and offers a way out of the consequences of sin.

For me it is best summarized in the words in 2 Peter:

"But do not forget this one thing, dear friends: with the Lord a day is like a thousand years, and a thousand years are like a day. The Lord is not slow in keeping his promise, as some understand slowness. He is patient with you, not wanting anyone to perish, but everyone to come to repentance. But the day of the Lord will come like a thief. The heavens will disappear with a roar; the elements will be destroyed by fire, and the earth and everything in it will be laid bare. Since everything will be destroyed in this way, what kind of people ought you to be? You ought to live holy and godly lives as you look forward to the day of God and speed its coming. That day will bring about the destruction of the heavens by fire, and the elements will melt in the heat. But in keeping with his promise we are looking forward to a new heaven and a new earth, the home of righteousness." (2 Peter 3:8-13, NIV)

What is going on in the world today in the area of sexual immorality and other things breaks the heart of God and He wants all to come to repentance but someday God will bring judgment and His judgment is final. Jesus says to the church – don't close your eyes to what is going on around you. Don't say it is okay when it is not.

Number 4: Hold on to what you have (Verses 24-25)

Jesus now addresses those in verse 19 that He commended earlier. To the ones who have not been sucked in by Jezebel He gives one thing for them to do: Hold on to what they have. What is that? Their deeds and their love and their faith and their service and their perseverance.

How do you "hold on"? Faithfulness in the Word - Faithfulness in Worship - Faithfulness in Prayer - Surrounding yourself by Godly people and advice - Feeding your mind on the things of God, not the things of the world.

Number 5: Live to claim His promises (Verses 26-29)

Here is a passage where scripture interprets scripture: 2 Tim 2:10-12 says, "So I am willing to endure anything if it will bring salvation and eternal glory in Christ Jesus to those God has chosen. This is a trustworthy saying: If we die with him, we will also live with him. If we endure hardship, we will reign with him." (2 Timothy 2:10-12, NIV) Those words from Paul go right along with the message of Revelation – if we endure, we will reign with Him.

In conclusion, have you ever gone through those boxes in the attic or the garage where you stored all of that stuff that you just couldn't let go. When doing that did you ever say to yourself, "Why did I hang on to that?"

I want you to stop and look at your life. I want you to take inventory and see if there are some things you have hung onto that probably aren't all that important.

Hold on to the things that matter to Jesus.

Dig Deeper: Questions to Consider from Chapter 2

If you're like us, there are items in chapter 2 that hit too close to home in our faith, our relationships with others, and our daily lives. Although some of these topics make us uncomfortable, they are necessary for us to grow and become better human beings. We all have heard the analogy between the need to challenge ourselves with the process required to make muscles stronger. Often times it's not fun working out or exercising to the point where our muscles grow, but it is necessary. The end product justifies the hard work of the process.

Take some time answering the questions below because growth requires honesty. When you're finished, share your answers with a trusted person. Perhaps you can grow together. Cheer up: This is the "easy" part of Revelation. It will only get more pointed and personal from here (sarcasm).

1. The church in Ephesus was taken down a couple of notches when Jesus told them that they should not get too comfortable in their faith. How about you? In what ways are you comfortable in your faith?

2. When the book you are reading was written, there wasn't too much of a parallel between society's handling of western religion and the suffering described in the letter to Smyrna. It appears to be coming (and if you are reading this book in the future, it very well could have already come). If you had to suffer for your faith, how would you suffer so as to be a beacon of hope to others?

3. The believers in Pergamum were forcefully told to Repent of the ways where they had strayed from the teachings of Jesus. Where have you strayed from the Gospel? What is required to be restored and compliant with the Scriptures?

4. And last but not least, Thyatira. We learned about tolerance versus compromise. How have you compromised your faith? How can you remedy those actions?

5. Are there any groups present in our society that Jesus would label as the Nicolaitans? Why? Why not?

Sardis

Background of Sardis

Sardis was a well-fortified city built high on a hill with mountain cliffs all around. They thought that no one could defeat them. They were so confident that they didn't even bother posting guards at the edge of the city walls. This over-confidence became their downfall and twice in their history they fell to an invading force. One would think that the population would have learned their lesson after the first time they were invaded, but history tells us that they did not learn their lesson. Apparently that complacency and over confidence had crept into the church at Sardis.

Sardis was also a wealthy city, actually one of the wealthiest in the area. One of their kings was such a wealthy man that he became the standard by which to judge wealth, saying that a person was "as wealthy as Croesus."

History teaches us that the people of Sardis were focused on the wrong things: wealth rather than security for example. As a result, the city disappeared and ceased to exist.

Jesus is the Ultimate Author of the Letter

"To the angel of the church in Sardis write: These are the words of him who holds the seven spirits of God and the seven stars." (Revelation 3:1, NIV)

At this point in the book, you now understand that at the beginning of each letter, John paints a portrait that Jesus is the ultimate author of the letter to the church. John may have put the pen on the paper and physically written the words, but Jesus spoke the words to him in the visions. You also at this point understand that the letters were addressed to "the angel" but that was likely a leader of the church. We will thus move on from continually pointing this out as we analyze the specific churches.

However, we do want to spend some time looking into whether the depiction of Jesus was used specifically to address the issues within this church. John attributes Jesus as the one who holds the "seven spirits of God and the seven stars". The phrase "seven spirits" is mentioned in three other times in Revelation and is understood to signify the omnipresence of God: He knows all because He is everywhere. The phrase "seven stars" is used three other times in Revelation and the phrase is understood to signify how the believers were to shine within their culture.

There is a parallel between the church in Sardis and the church in Ephesus because the "seven stars" phrase is used in the letter to both churches. Previously we discussed that the focus of the letter to Ephesus was how the church abandoned their relationship with Jesus. Use of the same phrase to the Sardis church portends a similar level of instruction. Indeed, the focus of the letter to the church in Sardis was one of complacency within the church. The Sardis believers were fine with doing the bare minimum, which doesn't line up with God's plan for His followers.

A Lack of Good Deeds

This was a scary position for the church in the early formation of the Christian religion. John writes in verse 4 that there are some believers in the church in Sardis who have kept to the faith, but it is reasonable to believe that these believers were the minority. The fact that the believers were being called out for a lack of action within the community is a scary position. As you will discover throughout the remainder of this chapter, Jesus has some harsh words and rebukes for believers who simply stopped putting their faith into action.

We believe there is also a parallel within modern society as well. If there is one characteristic predominant in society today, it is one of busyness. We are all busy working, focusing on children and their activities, working a side-hustle, taking care of aging parents, running errands, sleeping, spending time on our phones, etc. There simply doesn't seem to be enough time in the day to accomplish everything on our to-do list. As a result, we start to "de-clutter" our lives. Some stop going out and visiting with friends. Some stop spending time with the neighbors. And yes, some stop going to church. The result of all this culling of "non-essential" activities is that we increase our internal focus. Sure, we may still be involved at work, clubs, and other groups, but are we truly connecting with other people. We thrive when we focus on others rather than ourselves. We thrive when we reach out to others in their time of need.

Time for a mental checklist: If this letter was written to you, would there be a lack of good deeds upon which to heap praise on you?

Dead Inside

"I know your deeds; you have a reputation of being alive, but you are dead." *(Revelation 3:1, NIV)*

When we look at this church and compare it to the church in America today, it seems they may have a lot in common. The church at Sardis may be an example of the greatest threat facing the American church. Unlike some of the other churches we looked at, where persecution was an issue, there apparently was not a lot of persecution against the believers in Sardis. Perhaps this was because there was no distinction between the non-believers and the believers.

There was a saying many years ago that probably could have applied to the church in Sardis that went something like this: One of the worst things for believers is to go to church on Sunday to learn more about God but then deny Him with their lifestyle the rest of the week. The call to action from this saying was that your behavior is an indicator of your internal beliefs, thoughts, and convictions. As believers, we are called to show God to others. This is what the Bible refers to as being a light:

"You are the salt of the earth. But if the salt loses its saltiness, how can it be made salty again? It is no longer good for anything, except to be thrown out and trampled underfoot. You are the light of the world. A town built on a hill cannot be hidden. Neither do people light a lamp and put it under a bowl. Instead they put it on its stand, and it gives light to everyone in the house. In the same way, let your light shine before others, that they may see your good deeds and glorify your Father in heaven." (Matthew 5:13-16, NIV)

Everyone makes mistakes, even Christians. But what is important in this case, and in the case of our society today, is that there needs to be a recognition of these mistakes. Because repentance and correction can only occur after we acknowledge that we have messed up. But the issue with the believers in Sardis is that they thought they were doing just fine, typically called a "lack of self-awareness", something we are ALL guilty of, believers and non-believers. We volunteer to help at our children's school but fail to talk to the neighbor outside as we hustle from the car into the house. We have a reputation for being alive (volunteering) but are we really living?

Wake Up! And Repent!!!

"Wake up! Strengthen what remains and is about to die, for I have found your deeds unfinished in the sight of my God. Remember, therefore, what you have received and heard; hold it fast, and repent. But if you do not wake up, I will come like a thief, and you will not know at what time I will come to you." (Revelation 3:2-3, NIV)

The language of this letter is direct and focused on action that the believers in Sardis need to heed in order to return to their faith. There are many commands in this letter but we want to focus on three: wake up, strengthen, and repent. These commands are not only relevant for believers back in John's day, but also for believers and non-believers alike today.

Command #1: Wake up:

Have you ever seen someone sleepwalking? They appear to be going through the motions as if they were awake, but in reality are asleep, fully disconnected from the world around them. What is the response to someone sleepwalking? We shake them or speak to them in a loud voice to get them awake. Another example: when Roger wakes up in the morning, it requires a minimum of two alarms blasting loud music to get him to awake from his slumber. Look back to the first two words of this section: "Wake up!". Jesus is commanding the Sardis believers to get back to reality. Or, as we would say it in our culture, they needed to "wake up and smell the coffee."

Command #2: Strengthen what remains:

Jesus wants us to continually go deeper in our faith; we are expected to grow throughout our remaining time on Earth. But sometimes our faith can get stale. When this happens, we need to go back to the basics, to the beginning when that spark first ignited in our relationship with God. Once we reflect back, He says, "Hold it fast"

The first command is "Hold it fast". The Greek grammar for the phrase "Hold it fast" is a 2nd person imperative – a command that says, "Hey you. Yeah. You're the one I'm talking to – Hold on tightly to what you remember", but it also can be translated "strengthen it". Make it grow. So, when you reflect on that first encounter with God, hold on to it and then take it and let it help you grow. Take a verse like John 11:35 and realize that when Jesus wept it meant that He was human, yet divine. He cares for you. He knows your heart. He weeps over you when He sees you doing something you shouldn't, or He rejoices when you do something out of love for someone else.

Command #3: Repent

The second major command He gives us is "Repent". This is also a 2nd person imperative command. It is also saying, "Hey you! That's right. I'm talking to you – you need to admit to where you have messed up, where you have not done what is right." Repentance is saying to God, "I'm sorry that I made something else more important in my life than you God. God, your love is enough for me. I don't need that other thing in my life and I am sorry that I made that other thing more important." Repentance is turning from sin and dedicating yourself to living without sin.

Notice that the reward for following these commands isn't explicitly written in verse three. Instead, John records what is due to those who do not wake-up and change course in their faith. Punishment is the result. Attributing Jesus coming as a "thief in the night" does not signify a positive outcome if the believers in Sardis do not change their behavior.

For those that do repent, there is a glorious reward.

Reward for Good Deeds

"Yet you have a few people in Sardis who have not soiled their clothes. They will walk with me, dressed in white, for they are worthy. The one who is victorious will, like them, be dressed in white. I will never blot out the name of that person from the book of life, but will acknowledge that name before my Father and his angels." (Revelation 3:4-5, NIV)

Yes, the reward for the believers in Sardis that kept on with a living faith, and those that repented and changed course, was eternal life with Jesus in heaven. Let's focus on the imagery that is portrayed in this letter as it is more descriptive than other letters. First, Jesus says that the believers will "walk with him". With the exception of Jesus's 33 years on Earth, no one has had the privilege of walking with any aspect of God since Adam sinned in the Garden of Eden. Communing with the Creator of all life - what a glorious promise for us as we seek to thrive in our culture today!

Secondly, Jesus notes that the believers will be dressed in white as they are in His presence, communing with Him as they walk with Him. Throughout history the color white has been used to denote pureness. What a glorious promise that if we stay alive in our faith that all of our impurities will be erased when we are in heaven.

Finally, Jesus says that He will never erase in the book of life the names of those that stay alive in the faith. The phrase "book of life" refers to eternal life in heaven. What a glorious promise for us that we will live forever with Him in heaven! He goes on to say that He will represent that we are deserving of heaven to God, His father.

Roger's Ramblings: The Great Commission

"Then Jesus came to them and said, "All authority in heaven and on earth has been given to me. Therefore go and make disciples of all nations, baptizing them in the name of the Father and of the Son and of the Holy Spirit, and teaching them to obey everything I have commanded you. And surely I am with you always, to the very end of the age." (Matthew 28:18-20, NIV)

These are the last recorded words of Jesus before He ascended into heaven which tells us that the words and messages were (and are) important to Him. Earlier in this chapter we mentioned the parallel between the church in Sardis and churches in our world today. I think the comparison is spot-on, unfortunately, which is alarming because we live in a world that is increasingly becoming post-Christian. A spiritually dead church in a post-Christian world is not a good combination. If nothing else, the study of the church at Sardis provides precedence of this perilous position.

Jesus provided a perfect blueprint for the mission of churches, and by extension, of believers that are called by His name. The mission is simple: Go, Make Disciples, Baptize, Teach. Let's look at each:

Mission 1: Go….(into) all nations:

The first commandment to the church is to "go". While there are varying interpretations as to the implication of the word "go", there can be no doubt that believers are commanded to look outside of the church and minister to people. It is generally understood that there are four primary mission fields for churches: Community, Local, National, and International. The community is the area immediately around the church and/or believer. It is the neighborhood around the church. It is the people in your office. It is the people in your own neighborhood. The local mission field is your city and state. There are many opportunities for you to assist organizations that are actively going and reaching people for Christ. The same is true on a national level. Finally, contrary to our "America First" mentality, the need to hear and learn about Jesus is great in other countries and continents.

Churches that are alive are involved in reaching people in all four areas in order to make the greatest impact in sharing the news about Jesus with people. What can you do to "Go" reach others?

Mission 2: Make disciples

Churches are not social clubs. While it is true that there is an aspect of fellowship amongst believers, the church's primary mission is one other than getting together once a week to drink coffee in the fellowship hall. We are told to make "disciples". Remember from earlier that a disciple is someone who accepts and assists in spreading the doctrines of another, in this case Christ. Jesus tells us that we are called to create others that will in turn spread the message of Jesus to still more people.

The making of disciples involves preaching of the word and actually listening to the messages, adding them to our minds and thoughts. We must study on our own to learn more about what it means to live for Jesus (aka: be alive). We must apply what we've learned to our lives so that we will show others Jesus.

I would argue this was the primary task of the church in Sardis and now of churches in our world today. The church in Sardis died because the believers were spiritually dead and didn't want to change their ways. Churches today are dying, most likely for the same reasons. But take heart: There are umpteen churches today that continue to focus on making disciples and are still alive. If you're not attending one, find one of these churches.

Mission 3: Baptize

We humans sometimes tend to get tied up into issues of different understanding regarding doctrine as we seek to follow Christ. One of those areas is the issue of baptism. Is it required for salvation? Is it not? We will not get into theology here but it would seem that if Jesus commanded His followers to baptize people, that He had a reason for it.

Mission 4: Teach

This is another command that seems clear: Jesus tells us that we are called to teach everyone to "obey everything He has commanded us". We are all teachers. Often times we are scared when someone asks us about our faith because we don't want to stumble or not give the other person all the necessary information. Sometimes we are scared because we don't want to offend anyone else. However, that is not what we are instructed to do. Notice that Jesus doesn't say, "only teach when the person is already a believer and you are in a small group meeting". He didn't say, "only teach your immediate family members." No, He commanded us to teach everyone, whenever necessary. Who can you teach?

The reward for being a believer that is alive? Heaven, of course. But look what else Jesus promised: He will be with us forever. This seems like something we would all want, to have Jesus in our lives. Forever. What better encouragement to thrive amongst the chaos of our society that Jesus is walking everyday besides us during our time on this earth and into the next?

Let's learn from the early church as described in the book of Acts so that we don't end up like the church in Sardis. Once the Sardis church disappeared, there was no one to influence their community into a relationship with Jesus.

"They devoted themselves to the apostles' teaching and to fellowship, to the breaking of bread and to prayer. Everyone was filled with awe at the many wonders and signs performed by the apostles. All the believers were together and had everything in common. They sold property and possessions to give to anyone *who had need. Every day they continued to meet together in the temple courts. They broke bread in their homes and ate together with glad and sincere hearts, praising God and enjoying the favor of all the people. And the Lord added to their number daily those who were being saved." (Acts 2:42-47, NIV)*

Listen Up!

"Whoever has ears, let them hear what the Spirit says to the churches." (Revelation 3:6, NIV)

John's reminder to the church in Sardis to pay attention to the words in the letter is perhaps the strongest challenge of all the letters thus far. Like the passengers and crew on the Titanic, these believers were on a collision course with disaster and didn't realize it.

This wake-up call also applies to everyone in our society today: the longer you put off focusing on others, the harder it becomes to change course later in life. If you don't make the concerted effort today to take your co-worker that is going through a divorce out for coffee, the harder it will become to ever take that action.

Opportunities are presented every day. Learn to recognize them. And then act upon them.

Points to Ponder with Jeff: What You Need to Know

Just as Jesus is honest with His church, He wants His church to be honest with itself. As I stepped back and looked at this church and I asked, "What does Sardis have to do with us today?", I found myself saying, "A lot, and we really need to know how well Jesus knew His church then and now."

First, we need to know what He knows about us and not dismiss it:

It is too easy to dismiss things that we don't think matter or are not a threat to us. The church of Sardis made the mistake along the way of dismissing some things about their faithfulness to God.

What did Jesus know about the church at Sardis? What He knew didn't paint a very pretty picture. Evidently they looked good to the community, but it was just a facade. At some point they had started some good things but along the way what they were doing just faded away.

What could have caused that to happen in the church? Jesus says that there were some who had not "soiled their clothes", which implies that there were many who HAD soiled their clothes. Evidently many were influenced by others who did not follow God or do things that pleased God. They had one foot in the church and one foot in the world.

It could have been the culture of the city permeating the church – wealthy, self-reliant, always wanting to look good in front of others – I think that could have played a role. It could have been weak leadership in the church – leaders that did not focus enough on the things of God – I think that could have played a role.

What does this have to do with churches today? If we are not careful we can fall into the same trap the church at Sardis did. The church must care about the spiritual condition of the people in the church more than anything else. We can do things that look good in the community as a group but that is negated very quickly if the people of the church don't live like followers of Jesus in the community. I would rather be known as a church full of followers of Jesus living in the community rather than a church that "looks good" to the community.

Can I give an honest assessment where I believe churches need to grow? Most churches do a great job at offering opportunities to worship and learn throughout the week. But as the church is made up of people, the question must be asked, "How is your spiritual life?" I want to challenge you to grow in your personal Bible study. We need to grow in the area of prayer and seeking the Holy Spirit to guide us. We need to grow in the area of being multi-generational – ministering to the families and youth as well as adults across all demographics. We need to intentionally make disciples and develop leadership in all areas of the church

Second, we need to know what He commands and do it:

It is important to keep the commands of God. You will find this consistently throughout the word of God. I was recently reading in Joshua of the Old Testament and this passage jumped out at me. In Joshua 22, Joshua gives these parting words to the half-tribe of Manasseh as he sends them back to their homes after helping capture the land:

"But be very careful to keep the commandment and the law that Moses the servant of the Lord gave to you: to love the Lord your God, to walk in obedience to Him, to keep His commands, to hold fast to Him and to serve Him with all your heart and with all your soul." (Joshua 22:5, NIV)

They were getting ready to go back and settle into their daily lives. They were going to enjoy the fruit of their labor. But Joshua knew something: it is very easy to get to comfortable and forget to do the basic things that got them at that place in their life. He tells them to "keep on in your walk with God". Jesus gives a very similar message to those in Sardis and to us in verse 3: "Remember, therefore, what you have received and heard; hold it fast, and repent." (Revelation 3:3, NIV)

Remember what you have received and heard. Do you remember your early walk with God? For some reason I remember the first Bible verse I memorized. I was in the 6th grade and we had starting attending a new church. I sat down next to a friend from school and he said, "Hey, if you memorize a Bible verse you will get a piece of candy." I said, "I don't know any Bible verses." He said, "Memorize John 11:35". I said "Ok, what does it say?" He said, "Jesus wept." "That's it?" "Yep." "Okay, I can do that." I did and got my piece of candy!

Finally, you need to know what He promises and then go for it:

There is a story of the city falling. In the 5th century BC, Sardis ruled over all other Asian cities. But Cyrus, King of Persia began a series of conquests and looked westward to the city of Sardis. Cyrus attacked the city several times without success. Just when Cyrus was about to give up, one of his soldiers spotted a Sardis soldier who had dropped his helmet down the slopes of the cliff on which the city was built. He watched the soldier climb down to get his helmet and then watched how he got back to the top. The king of Sardis was so confident in his position that he didn't feel the need to post guards! Cyrus, upon hearing what his soldier had seen, ordered his army to attack the city by going up that same path. Sardis was caught completely off guard and was defeated by a surprise attack.

Jesus wanted them to know that their confidence would lead to the same thing that happened to the city. He provides three promises:

1. Jesus's first promise is that He will return. Jesus's primary teaching on His return was this: you don't know when I will return. He even used the same imagery as a thief in the night to communicate this message. Be ready. Be found doing what I have asked you to do.

2. His second promise is that we will walk with Him in a white robe of victory. It was customary in the Jewish faith and then in the Christian faith in the early church to enter worship with a white robe. That image is also in Revelation 6 where those who had been slain for their faith were given a white robe and told to wait until the final judgment. The white robe symbolizes eternal life – the gift that He will give us.

3.　　His third promise is that those who are faithful will not have their names blotted out of the book of life. Jesus will be faithful to those who are faithful to Him.

Conclusion:

God gives what He promises. Here is a great verse from Joshua 21:45 (NIV): "Not one of all the Lord's good promises to Israel failed, every one was fulfilled." This comes after several chapters of listing all the boundaries of the properties that were given to the Israelites after they crossed over the Jordan river.

They didn't just walk in and take the land. They had to fight for the land. They had to work for it. They had to make sacrifices along the way. But in the end what was the result? Not one of the Lord's promises failed.

That in essence is the message of Revelation. There is a promised land waiting for you. Hang in there, remain faithful, follow His commands – and when you do – you've got eternal life waiting for you.

Philadelphia

Background of Philadelphia

Philadelphia was a smaller town just about 30 miles southeast of Sardis and was the youngest of all the cities addressed. It was founded in 189 BC by either King Eumenes or his brother Attalis II. They both ruled the city and historians are not sure which one founded the city. What we do know is that the name Philadelphia was given to the city because of the brother's profound love and loyalty for each other. We are familiar with a city in the US with that name, Philadelphia, the city of brotherly love. The name comes from the Greek words for brother (Adelphos) and love (Phileo).

The city was considered the "Gateway to the East", just like we refer to St. Louis as the "Gateway to the West". Attalus II had a mission for the city: to help spread the Greek way of life and culture. He was very successful: even though Rome conquered the known world at that time, the Greek language and culture dominated almost every region.

Picture of Jesus

"To the angel of the church in Philadelphia write: These are the words of him who is holy and true, who holds the key of David. What he opens no one can shut, and what he shuts no one can open." (Revelation 3:7, NIV)

"Holy". "True". "Holds the key of David." "What he opens no one can shut..." Jesus uses these words and phrases to describe Himself specifically for the believers in Philadelphia. Just as the believers were doing a good job, Jesus reminds them (and us) that they still fall short of a Holy God. The church needed to continue to pursue a Holy God so they need to pay attention to this letter.

Jesus described Himself as "true" to contradict all the other messages in the public arena in Philadelphia where other people were proclaiming themselves as a suitable replacement to God. This, of course, ties right in with being holy because the end product is the same. If something is holy, it is without defect. If something is true, it is without defect.

The phrase "holds the keys of David" would have gotten the attention of the believers because the Jewish religion played a key role during that day. The believers, as well as people around the world, would have recognized who David was and the power of his kingdom. Jesus is in effect saying that He was (is) greater than David ever was or could have hoped to be during his time on Earth. This communicates the power of Jesus to the believers in Philadelphia and would have encouraged them to remain strong in the faith.

Notice though, nothing in the introduction to the church was negative. It was all positive.

Good Job

"I know your deeds. See, I have placed before you an open door that no one can shut. I know that you have little strength, yet you have kept my word and have not denied my name." (Revelation 3:8, NIV)

This is the second time where Jesus reminds the church that He knows everything, including what they were doing to strengthen their faith and increase the spread of the Gospel. By now, we should all realize that there are no secrets from Jesus. This isn't like when we told a little lie to our parents while growing up because we didn't want to get into trouble. Some of us worked really hard to make sure that our parents never discovered the truth. Some are probably still having to keep the lie alive.

Jesus knows everything: our strengths, our weaknesses, our successes, our failures, our deepest, darkest secret, everything. Every. Thing. Is there relevance for us today? Absolutely. Let's focus on doing good: reaching out to people, comforting those we know going through a bad time, encouraging friends down on their luck, and helping others as they navigate through life. We'll make mistakes, but admit them to God, ask for forgiveness, and move on. Don't spend mental or emotional energy trying to hide something from God. That just won't work.

But, there is a warning in this message as well. Notice that Jesus didn't tell the believers to throw a party or to pat themselves on the back because they were so awesome. We need to be satisfied with the knowledge that what we do for others is the right thing to do for them and for ourselves. Recognition may come sometimes. We just need to do it for the Glory of God, knowing that He sees us.

From there, Jesus recognized the believers for keeping His word. It is easy to listen to someone but forget what they say. It is easy to read something but to forget what was written. It takes concentration and a dedicated effort to put what we have learned into practice. The believers in Philadelphia weren't perfect. But they were pushing forward in their attempt to keep His word. We need to take this promise to heart: What we do in the shadows is noticed by God.

Finally, Jesus recognized the believers for not denying His name. This sounds curious, especially to anyone not familiar with the story of Peter denying Jesus shortly before His death on the cross. How would have the early believers denied Jesus's name? This was likely a characteristic of the church in Sardis. They claimed to be followers of Jesus but they had let their faith slip to the point where they were indistinguishable from non-believers. They knew the truth but didn't take it to heart and put it into practice. This is denying Jesus's name. After the previous admonitions by Jesus for the believers in Philadelphia, it is no wonder that they wouldn't fall into this trap.

The Hour of Trial

"I will make those who are of the synagogue of Satan, who claim to be Jews though they are not, but are liars — I will make them come and fall down at your feet and acknowledge that I have loved you. Since you have kept my command to endure patiently, I will also keep you from the hour of trial that is going to come on the whole world to test the inhabitants of the earth." (Revelation 3:9-10, NIV)

On first glance, this passage seems vexing, at least for those who are referred to in the passage. But who exactly are these people who claim to be Jews but are in fact not Jews? It would appear that whoever they are, they are aligned against Jesus and should therefore not be emulated by anyone, either back then or today. Let's explore what we know to discover who Jesus opposes in Philadelphia.

We know that satan is against Jesus. He has been against God (and therefore by extension, Jesus) since before the creation of man. Furthermore, we know that there were two "kinds" of Jews back in the time of John: Jews that had accepted Jesus and followed Him and Jews that rejected Jesus as their Messiah. This passage is addressed to the second category of Jews, those who rejected Jesus. The text of this letter seems to indicate that Jesus sees no difference between satan and the non-believing Jews. They both are anti-Jesus.

With this as the background, the passage about those who will fall down at the feet of the believers in Philadelphia is a foreshadowing of Jesus's return. Everyone, believers and non-believers, will bow down at His feet. This was meant to provide encouragement to the believers while they were facing attacks from the non-believing Jews in Philadelphia. In fact, Jesus goes one step further and reassures the believers that their faithfulness will enable them to avoid trials and tribulations during the end times.

Some might argue that we are in the end times today. In view of recent geopolitical events, those people may not be wrong. But in a larger sense, we have been living in the last days ever since Jesus went back to heaven. When that day comes, will you be among the group falling at the feet of the believers (in other words, the non-believers) or will you be among the believers?

We are reminded of a scene in one of the Indiana Jones movies when the hero is fighting with a bad guy and they are both at risk of being sucked into a ship's moving propeller. The bad guy says that his soul is prepared to die and then asks whether Dr. Jones has the same confidence. That's a good question for us: Is your soul prepared?

Where is the Call to Repentance?

If it were possible (or permissible) to rank the "spiritual-ness" of the seven churches, the believers in Philadelphia would rank high on the list. They appeared to be living true to their faith, carrying out the great commission. Given what we have learned in the preceding verses then, it is no surprise that there is no "You need to repent" section in the letter to the church in Philadelphia. Its a good place to be in, because Jesus goes right to their reward.

The Reward

"I am coming soon. Hold on to what you have, so that no one will take your crown. The one who is victorious I will make a pillar in the temple of my God. Never again will they leave it. I will write on them the name of my God and the name of the city of my God, the new Jerusalem, which is coming down out of heaven from my God; and I will also write on them my new name." (Revelation 3:11-12, NIV)

We believe that Jesus allocated the largest amount of depictions of heaven in the letter to the church in Philadelphia for a specific reason. (We know, right now you're saying to yourself, "brilliant deduction, Captain Obvious". But hear us out) The church was oppressed, both from the Roman government and from non-believing Jews. But despite this severe opposition, the believers stood firm and true to their faith. They took their faith seriously. They deserved to have a higher insight into what awaited them in glory.

Read the passage again and notate all the references to heaven:

- "Crown" - The believers will rule with God in heaven.
- "One who is victorious" - Speaks to the importance of the believers holding true to their faith and overcoming the world.
- "Pillar" - Strong buildings require strong foundations. Architecture in their time would have relied on pillars to ensure that buildings didn't collapse.
- "Temple of my God" - Throughout the book of Revelation we are told that the dwelling place of God is with men. There is no longer any need for a divide in the temple between God and man that was due to incompatibility between a holy God and sinful man.
- "Never again will they leave it" - Forever. They will be with God forever. For. Ever.
- "New Jerusalem" - Jerusalem in their time was considered as a holy city, but it was full of sin and debauchery. The new Jerusalem would be the perfect home for a perfect God and the believers would be able to live with God.

Perseverance almost always brings about a reward. Ask any Navy Seal that perseveres through the entire selection process their view on the outcome of perseverance. Ask a marathon runner or elite cyclist whether perseverance is worth it in the end. Where in your life could you improve your perseverance?

Pay Attention

"Whoever has ears, let them hear what the Spirit says to the churches." *(Revelation 3:13, NIV)*

Each of the letters to the seven churches are important. This explains the presence of this command at the conclusion of each of the letters. But with all that we have learned regarding the believers in Philadelphia, you can't help but wonder if this was written with all-capital letters, bold font, underlined, or some other indicator for the angel of the church. You can almost hear John say to himself while he is writing this letter, "This is serious! Read it. Then read it again."

Remember what Paul said to Timothy: "I have fought the good fight, I have finished the race, I have kept the faith. Now there is in store for me the crown of righteousness, which the Lord, the righteous Judge, will award to me on that day—and not only to me, but also to all who have longed for his appearing." (2 Timothy 4:7-8, NIV).

Whoever has ears....

Points to Ponder with Jeff: Power & Possibilities, Perseverance & Promises

This church at Philadelphia is believed to be a small church. This is assumed from Jesus's description of it as "not having much strength." It was a church that seemingly would be overlooked by many people yet it had a special place in the heart of Jesus. Jesus doesn't judge the church by it's size but rather by it's heart. His message to them and to us is one of encouragement and promise. I've summarized His message in two phrases: Power and Possibilities & Perseverance and Promises. Let's look first at the Power and Possibilities

Power is seen in the person of Jesus

In verse 7, John attests to the fact that the authorship of the letter is Jesus. Like Athens, Philadelphia was a place with many temples and gave the emperor the title "The Son of the Holy One." Yet Jesus has the power of truth - Notice the play on words as Jesus describes Himself - "He who is holy, who is true" in verse 7; this is done to communicate His worthiness compared to emperor.

He is also described as the one who holds the key of David. David was seen as the greatest king in the history of Israel. He was the most powerful king they ever had. Jesus is the one who holds all that authority in His hand. He was far greater than the greatest king Israel had ever known. That last phrase really confirms the concept of His power: "What he opens no one can shut, and what he shuts no one can open."

We need to recognize the power and authority of Jesus in the church today. He is still King of Kings and Lord of Lords. John 1:1 tells us that He was in the beginning when all things were created. John 14 says He is "the way, the truth and the life." In Rev 1:18 He is the one who holds "the keys of death and Hades." Finally, in Acts 4:12, "Salvation is found in no one else, for there is no other name under heaven given to men by which we must be saved." (NIV)

Our prayer should be, "Lord, help us recognize and live by your power."

The Possibilities before His church

Philadelphia was founded with the intention that it might be a missionary of Greek culture and language to Lydia and Phrygia. It worked so well that by AD 19 the Lydians had forgotten their own language and were all but Greek.

That idea of mission in Philadelphia is what Jesus means when He speaks of the open door that is set before Philadelphia. Now there has come to it another great missionary opportunity, an open door to carry to men who never knew it the message of the love of Jesus Christ.

God has placed His church in a unique time and place. We need to grow in our outreach to the community. We need to grow in our retention and assimilation of new people. If we have results in those areas, then think about all of the new people that will come into a saving, eternal relationship with Jesus. What is the key to all of that? Do what the church of Philadelphia did: "you have kept my word and have not denied my name."

That is just scratching the surface of the power of Jesus and the possibilities that He has put before us. I want to challenge you to make all of this a matter of prayer. What does God have in store for His church today?

Jesus doesn't stop there. He goes on to talk about perseverance and promises.

Perseverance gives the Promise of Power over your enemies

Who were the enemies of the Christians there? Ironically, again, they faced more opposition from the Jews than the Roman government. But look what Jesus says about those that will oppose the Christians. They will be humbled. They will bow down and acknowledge that God loves them.

The impact of that statement challenged the Jews because they could not accept that God would love anyone else but them. But Jesus says they would bow down and have to acknowledge that Jesus even loves the Gentiles. Why would all of this happen? Because they "kept my command to endure patiently." This goes along with the passage in Philippians which says, "that at the name of Jesus every knee should bow, in heaven and on earth and under the earth, and every tongue confess that Jesus Christ is Lord, to the glory of God the Father." (Philippians 2:10-11, NIV)

Jesus will take care of His children in the end. It does not mean that we will not have bad days and suffer at times for what we believe in, but in the end – We Win! This is just another reinforcement of the purpose of the book of Revelation: encouragement to remain faithful until the day Jesus returns and judgment is brought to the world.

Perseverance gives the Promise of Protection

The passage from verse 10-11 is definitely a picture of the end times. I don't know all of the details and what is all going to happen but Jesus says here that He will give protection from the hour of trial. Revelation points to a time when there will be a final conflict. This may be a reference to that time.

The promise is that those who hold on to their faith will be protected during that time and no one will be able to take the crown of life from them. The crown, a symbol of victory.

Perseverance Gives the Promise of stability

Verses 12-13 give a picture of strength and stability. The image of a "pillar" was very vivid in the ancient world. I've been fortunate to have visited many historical ruins during my life. The one thing that seems to survive in ancient ruins is pillars – almost every picture of ruins you see has pillars in it. A pillar is a support, something which holds steady that around it. What a great promise to those who lived in constant turmoil from an unsteady and unpredictable earth, that they themselves would become a solidifying, steadying force.

The church at Philadelphia took to heart what Jesus said and thrived. They must have loved the image of being a pillar because there are many pillars among the ruins that have been excavated in the city.

Perseverance Promises a new identity

Jesus says a "new name" will be given. Philadelphia understood that imagery also. The city received a new name twice in the first century: the first time after a massive earthquake in AD 17. In fact, it was so decimated that it was designated "Neocaesarea" in gratitude for Tiberius' generosity to help rebuild the city. The second time in the early 70's it was designated "Flavia" after Vespasian gave financial assistance following a similar catastrophe.

Name changes in the Bible were significant. They usually marked a big change or event in someone's life. Jesus uses that imagery to emphasize the change that will occur when He returns. A new name will be given to those who endure to the end.

So, what will remaining faithful to Jesus get you? Power over your enemies. Protection over the "hour of trial. Stability. And, last but not least, a new identity.

I don't know about you, but that all sounds like a pretty good deal. Especially since none of it is temporary – its for eternity.

Laodicea

Background of Laodicea

The city of Laodicea was located on an elevated position between mountain ranges. Similar to other ancient cities, it was located near water. In this case, Laodicea was located between the rivers Asopus and Caprus, which emptied into the larger Lycus River. The strategic location meant that Laodicea was in the middle of several major trade routes. As we have seen in previous discussions about other churches in Revelation, the proximity to trade routes equated to a wealthy population. Their wealth was such that Laodicea was known throughout the Roman empire as an extremely rich city. In fact, in AD 61 an earthquake destroyed the city and they turned down the financial help from Rome.

But the Laodicean's wealth did not all come from trade. The city was also highly regarded throughout the Roman empire for its linen and wool industry. Laodicea produced high quality cloth and carpets, especially from the glossy black wool of sheep raised in the area. Perhaps it is no surprise then that the city was also known as a center for health and wellness. Its medical school and medicines, notable among which was an eye-ointment made from a powder produced in Phrygia, were widely famed across Asia.

Perhaps the most relevant aspect of the city, at least for our study of John's letter, was the way in which they received water. One would think that being in close proximity to three rivers, that the rivers would have been a source for water. This was not the case however. The city of Laodicea had a water system that brought water from hot springs some 5 miles away. By the time it got to them it had cooled down enough that it was drinkable but still lukewarm.

Laodicea continued to have a prominent place in Christianity after receiving John's letter. In fact, the city became the site of leadership when a bishop was appointed to one of the churches in the city. Interestingly enough, archaeologists estimate that there were as many as 20 churches in the city. Later, the city would host a council of leaders in the Christian religion. Christianity continued to be strong in the city until an earthquake destroyed the city in the seventh century and the city was abandoned.

We mention the history of the church in Laodicea after John's letter because it indicates that the believers took the message of the letter to heart and changed their behavior. There is always hope for anyone to change their ways. Redemption is always possible.

The Final Picture of Jesus in the Letters

"To the angel of the church in Laodicea write: These are the words of the Amen, the faithful and true witness, the ruler of God's creation." (Revelation 3:14, NIV)

When the leader of the church in Laodicea opened the letter, he was not going to have a good day. We all get defensive when we receive correction, and his church was about to get a lot of correction. It would have been understandable if he would have burned the letter after reading how the church had drifted from its mission.

As a result, Jesus needed to immediately get their attention. Once He had their attention, He needed to ensure that they paid attention to the words and message of the letter. He accomplishes this task perfectly in this letter introduction:

- "The words of the Amen" - These words speak to the finality of God. The usage of the phrase "Alpha and Omega" was used to convey that God was, is, and always will be. Consider Paul's words in 2 Corinthians: "But as surely as God is faithful, our message to you is not 'Yes' and 'No.' For the Son of God, Jesus Christ, who was preached among you by us—by me and Silas and Timothy—was not 'Yes' and 'No,' but in him it has always been 'Yes.' For no matter how many promises God has made, they are 'Yes' in Christ. And so through him the 'Amen' is spoken by us to the glory of God. Now it is God who makes both us and you stand firm in Christ. He anointed us, set his seal of ownership on us, and put his Spirit in our hearts as a deposit, guaranteeing what is to come." (2 Corinthians 1:18-22, NIV)

- "The faithful and true witness" - Jesus is always faithful and can always be trusted. His words are "true" because He speaks for God the Father. What Jesus is about to say is an accurate representation of what God has to say to the church in Laodicea.
- "Ruler of God's creation" - As wholly God, Jesus has been given all power in heaven and on Earth. His authority over His kingdom surpasses any type of authority any man could claim on the church, including the leaders of the church, the Jews, and yes, even the Romans.

The believers need to pay attention to the letter and do what it says.

Where is the Praise??

We first saw this deviation from the letter pattern in the previous chapter, the letter to the church in Philadelphia. But this time, the missing content is not the bad behavior that is in need of correction. Nothing good is mentioned. The letter starts hopeful with the phrase, "I know your deeds", but apparently there were no good deeds on that list.

Before we move on to the long, the very long, list of behaviors that needed to be corrected with the believers in Laodicea, let's pause for a time of personal reflection. As you will read, the Laodicean believers are going to be held accountable for being lukewarm, that is, neither hot nor cold. If someone looked at your life, would they consider you lukewarm? Whether you are a believer or not, the mental exercise is important. Do you consider yourself hot? We do not mean in the physical sense, nor do we mean hot in the temperature sense.

One of the favorite exercises for human resource departments during recent years is to have workers perform a self evaluation prior to annual performance reviews. The alleged purpose is to determine whether there is a disconnect between how the worker views their performance compared to how their supervisor views the same worker's performance. (We say alleged because we are confident that the real intent behind this exercise is to reduce the workload of the supervisor and the HR department. But we digress.) Imagine that you are preparing for a review of your ability to thrive during the chaos of our society today. Would you give yourself a high rating (ie: "hot")? A low rating (ie: "cold")? Or are you lukewarm? How does your rating compare to what a friend or family member would rate you?

The reason for this exercise is to prepare for the coming sections. We often think more highly of ourselves than we actually are. This sounds very similar to the church in Laodicea: they falsely believed that their deeds were good when in reality they were at substantial risk. Let's be honest with ourselves so that we have an accurate starting point. If we are lukewarm, let's own it and read on to learn how to become hot again.

The List of Bad Behavior is Long...

"I know your deeds, that you are neither cold nor hot. I wish you were either one or the other! So, because you are lukewarm—neither hot nor cold—I am about to spit you out of my mouth. You say, 'I am rich; I have acquired wealth and do not need a thing.' But you do not realize that you are wretched, pitiful, poor, blind and naked." (Revelation 3:15-17, NIV)

The list of behaviors where the believers in Laodicea fell short was long but can be summarized as this: they had a mindset problem. Reading the text above, it is reasonable to assume that the church believed that their faith was sufficient. This is not surprising; as citizens of one of the wealthiest cities throughout the Roman empire, they would have been wealthy as well.

It is human nature that when we "make it", we believe that the hard work is finished and we can coast throughout life. Just look at the countless number of football, baseball, or basketball prospects that come highly rated out of college but then amount to little in the professional leagues. We are never good enough. Our work to improve the lives of others is never sufficient. We must constantly be striving to be better. Unfortunately, the church in Laodicea did not subscribe to this philosophy.

Describing something as sufficient or good enough is the equivalent of calling food or a beverage lukewarm. Indeed, this is the first characteristic of the church that Jesus takes issue with in the letter to Laodicea. There are two issues with the church: their deeds and their mindset.

Their deeds:

The phrase "neither cold nor hot" speaks to how the believers were nothing like what was desired for people that followed Christ. The imagery here is food or drink. When we eat or drink something, the desire is that it is either cold or hot, but not in between. When was the last time that you sat down for dinner and enjoyed a lukewarm meal? Perhaps you worked late and by the time you got home mealtime was over but the food was still warming in the oven. Did it taste the same as it would have if you made it home earlier? Or, in perhaps the gravest tragedy: lukewarm French fries at your favorite fast food restaurant. Why do these get passed on to the customer? Just throw them away! We'll wait for hot fries. Don't even get us started about lukewarm ice cream shakes.

The same imagery that you are conjuring up right now would have been the same for the believers in Laodicea. Because the system that transported the water to the city was a great distance, the cold water pulled from the spring was lukewarm when it reached the city. They definitely understood how undesirable water was that was lukewarm when something cold was desired. Cold beverages are refreshing. Hot beverages are relaxing. Lukewarm beverages are neither.

When Jesus said that their deeds are lukewarm, it wasn't a positive affirmation of their behavior. It is reasonable to conclude that the believers were not making a positive impact on Laodicea. What did this look like? Probably the opposite of how the early church was described in Acts 2:42-47 (NIV):

- No devotion to the apostles' teaching, fellowship, breaking of bread, and prayer.
- Lack of awe at wonders and signs performed by the apostles.
- Were not together and didn't have everything in common.
- Didn't sell property and possessions to give to anyone who had need.
- Didn't meet every day.
- Didn't meet together to break bread or eat together with glad and sincere hearts.

- Didn't praise God.
- Didn't enjoy the favor of all the people.

The result? Lives were not being changed and very likely, people were not added to the number of those being saved.

What are some of the ways that your deeds are lukewarm? Whether you are a believer or not, your deeds must not be lukewarm if you desire to thrive amidst the chaos of today.

Their mindset:

Jesus actually provides a snapshot into the mindset of the believers in verse 17 when He quotes them as saying, "I am rich; I have acquired wealth and do not need a thing." (Revelation 3:17, NIV). Indeed, the people within Laodicea probably were wealthy when compared to the inhabitants of surrounding cities. The believers were likely traders or involved with the linen trade. They may have even been involved in the medical industry. From a material and earthly perspective, they probably were indeed rich.

But spiritually, they were not rich. The words of Jesus sound harsh, but they were necessary for Him to drive the point that the believers needed to repent of their behavior. Consider the following:

- Wretched - Webster's on-line dictionary defines this word as "deeply afflicted, dejected, or distressed in body or mind; extremely or deplorably bad or distressing; being or appearing mean, miserable, or contemptible; very poor in quality or ability." Enough said: This is not something to which we should strive.
- Pitiful - Let's use Webster again. The on-line dictionary defines this word as, "deserving or arousing pity or commiseration; exciting pitying contempt". Well, that didn't help too much. Let's look at how the word "pity" is defined: "sympathetic sorrow for one suffering, distressed, or unhappy." Yep. We don't want to be considered as pitiful.
- Poor - This was probably used in a direct contradiction to how the believers viewed themselves. They thought they were rich but instead were the opposite.

- Blind - This speaks to the lack of growth in their faith. They were blind to their surroundings. We would refer to it as they lacked seeing the world through the eyes of Jesus.
- Naked - Clothing is used throughout the Bible to signify a relationship with God. By saying that the Laodiceans were naked, Jesus is saying that they didn't actually have a relationship with God.

Observation of our society and others around the world indicates that it is challenging for those that are wealthy to self-realize issues and implement correction. Yes, hard work was required throughout the process of obtaining that material status, but somewhere along the line the passion for continued improvement is forgotten. Wealth, possessions, and status have been achieved and life is good enough.

Perhaps an example from the sports world will bring clarity to this point. Roger is a huge fan of soccer. He has played hundreds, if not thousands, of games of soccer. He has coached youth teams through hundreds of games. He has watched hundreds of games of soccer on the television. He has attended many professional matches from the collegiate level to the highest professional levels. He is, in a word, obsessed. One of his frustrations deals with the inability of the United States Men's National Soccer Team to perform at the highest level in the World Cup. No matter our talent level, the national team struggles to get out of the group level at the premier global soccer tournament. His constant refrain is how in the world can we not get a team of the best players in the world from a country of 350 million people?

There are a myriad of reasons, of course, but chief among them is hunger. Not physical hunger, but a deep-down yearning to improve one's life that leads to an insanely high level of desire. This hunger is generally missing from our society, which ultimately is very good because even the poorest amongst our society are richer than many in other countries. But this standard of living provides opportunity to fall back upon in case of failure. To succeed in the highest level of soccer in the US, one must start the child playing soccer almost as soon as they can walk. Then once they have demonstrated they can walk and run with a soccer ball, they are whisked away from the recreational league to join a competitive (traveling) team. The thought is that in order to advance, the child must play higher level of competition. This will then require hundreds, if not thousands, of dollars spent per year, not to mention the many hours, to get the child to play competitively. Needless to say, this system eliminates highly talented players that cannot afford these fees or parents that cannot afford the time commitment. As a result, we eliminate a plethora of players that could be more talented than those on national team rosters.

Contrast that system with other countries. On one of his trips to Rio de Janeiro, Brazil, Roger was taking a taxi to the airport. As they drove past a very poor section of town, known as a favela, the driver communicated that Ronaldo, one of the best players to come out of Brazil, grew up in that poor neighborhood. What drove Ronaldo? The hunger to change his life and get out of that favela. He was the poorest among the poor and became one of the best players in the world.

What does that have to do with Laodicea and our desire to thrive amidst the chaos of our society? Read what Jesus had to say about the issue in Matthew: "Then Jesus said to his disciples, 'Truly I tell you, it is hard for someone who is rich to enter the kingdom of heaven. Again I tell you, it is easier for a camel to go through the eye of a needle than for someone who is rich to enter the kingdom of God.'" (Matthew 19:23-24, NIV).

Wealth is not bad. But the mindset can be bad. What is your mindset? Do you have a hunger to thrive?

Roger's Ramblings: A Testament to a Father's Love

One of life's biggest annoyances is biting into dinner recently microwaved where a hot and delicious outside hides the fact that the core of the food remains completely frozen. There are about 2-3 bites of hot food but then it quickly switches to lukewarm temperature and then finally to a cold, frozen mess. As soon as you bite into the lukewarm food, the realization that the meal is going to be subpar brings disappointment. It also brings a choice: do you soldier on and eat the cold food? Do you put it back into the microwave and wait a few more minutes? Or do you simply throw it away?

There are a myriad of other situations where food should either be cold or hot, but not in between. Cold is desirable at times such as a refreshing beverage on a sunny day, ice cream, or a Popsicle. I am a self-designated connoisseur of Mountain Dew and nothing beats a refreshing glass-bottle of Mountain Dew.

Lukewarm Dew is not nearly as satisfying and borders on gross. I'll still drink it, but I will be wishing that it was cold the entire time. Another part of life that needs to be cold is the room temperature at night for sleeping. Burrowing under the covers is superior to sleeping in a warm room. Sleep quality always seems better in a cold room than in a lukewarm room.

Other times, hot is desirable. Hot chocolate, properly cooked foods, and hot tea all must be hot to activate the proper taste buds. Coffee also must be hot (or so I've heard as I've never had a cup). My coffee-loving friends tell me that lukewarm coffee is trash.

What's the point? Just as Jesus had trouble with the church in Laodicea, so is the concept of lukewarm similarly viewed in our time. We can point to things outside us that should be hot or cold. But what about our lives and actions? Are there any areas in our lives where we are lukewarm?

In 2005, my Dad and I were discussing the state of the church in society. We were discouraged that many churches had forgotten their mission to save the lost (non-believers) and instead focused on their own internal wants and desires. So we decided to do something about it. We formed a business that we would use to communicate Biblical truth to people. We named the business Rev315 out of the letter to the church in Laodicea: "I know your deeds, that you are neither cold nor hot. I wish you were either one or the other!" (Revelation 3:15, NIV). We even created a website.

We got to work creating content. Both Dad and I wrote quite a few essays that we uploaded to the website. Dad focused on his strengths of standardizing organizational processes to increase the operational effectiveness. He wanted to help churches become more organized so that they could spend more time in evangelism efforts. My goal was to provide content to believers warning them of the consequences of being lukewarm. Two of our first essays can be found below.

"The Room"

The room was dark with no windows. It had a strong pungent odor which bordered on being overwhelming. The walls were the original speckled green and white when the foundation of the basement was finished sixty years ago. The room had been used as a storage space for all those items no one wanted but were to hesitant to discard. Large air vents were hanging from the ceiling along with a huge metal casement containing an air conditioning system which left a very low ceiling. No one wanted to use the room. To everyone, the room was very undesirable and a place to avoid.

There was one exception. Someone could see beyond the ugliness of the room and envisioned what it could be. He made the request to use the room as his office. Sure, why not, was the response. No one else would ever want to use the room. With diligent effort he began to clean up the room and even saw that the venting system was no longer needed. As he worked, the room changed into a functional office. What was once useless was transformed into something useful; it only took someone who could see beyond the visible and envision the invisible. Someone who took action to create a "new room" from the "old".

What do we, as Christians, see when we look at non-Christians. Do we only see the visible ugliness of worldly desires or do we see the beauty of what a person could be in Christ. Do we take action to create the "new" from the "old". Or are we like most who only see a "room" to avoid?

Bruce Vander Kolk
September 26, 2003

Lip Service

The opening lyrics to DC Talk's song "What if I stumble" as found on their album "Jesus Freak" are very telling and really speak to one of the core tenets here at Rev315: Our walk needs to match our talk. This belief is so important to us that we have coined a new term, "Lip Service". Too often we Christians think that all we have to do is to believe in God and go to church; what we fail to accept is that our responsibility continues when we step outside of the church building. But this is not a new problem. Read what John wrote in Revelation 3:14-22.

If you've spent any time on this site, you will notice something familiar with this passage: it is also the name of our company. Since we have analyzed the significance of this passage elsewhere in this website, we don't want to spend too much time discussing the passage of scripture here; we'd rather define what we mean by "lip service".

We define "lip service" as the practice by many Christians to accept Jesus with their words but not with their actions. You know who we're talking about (hopefully we're not talking about you, but if we are, there's still time to change your mind). The people who think all they have to do is go to church. We are speaking of people that go to church on Sundays, know all of the words to the songs, know when to stand, know what words to say during the service, are friendly with people at church, etc. These are the same people that undergo a 180 degree change in attitude when they leave the church building. They have one face for Sundays and one for the other six days of the week. In fact, they often hear the comment "I didn't know you went to church" and don't think anything of it.

Too often we are guilty of just giving lip service. Let's face it: whether we want to actually do it or not, it's just easier putting on a "church" face on Sundays and then blending in with the rest of the world the other six days of the week. We don't have to worry about saying something that people won't like or be offended at. We don't have to worry about being different from everyone else and risk any embarrassment when people laugh at us. If we pretend to be like everyone else, then we can blend in, be liked by everyone, be one of the cool crowd. Honestly, admit it: who wouldn't like to be liked and accepted by others? The only problem with that way of thinking though is that I just can't find the portion of scripture in the Bible where Jesus tells us to act different when we're in the world.

In fact, the I can only find Bible passages where Jesus tells us to act the same every day of the week as we do on Sundays. Consider these passages:

- James 2:14-26
- Matthew 25:31-46

Now, I'm not what you would call a biblical scholar, but it seems clear that "walking the talk" was very important to Jesus. Not only did He talk about it during His ministry, but His disciples also carried on the theme in their ministry. In order to truly accept the importance of this message, I think we need to discover why it was (and is) so important to Him. People aren't going to listen to what you have to say or what you believe in unless you really believe in it. And how do you show them you really believe in something? By doing it, everyday. How can we expect someone to believe in God if we don't even live our daily lives like we believe in God? They won't. Take environmentalists for example. Suppose an environmentalist tries to convince you to treat the earth better because of global warming. They tell you that you are polluting the environment with your motorcycle, your bulldozer, your semi truck, your SUV, etc., because of all the greenhouse gases they create. They have a pretty sound argument, right? But what if after telling you all this, they drive away in their SUV? Do they truly believe their message? Are you more or less likely to join their movement? If you're normal, then you would be less inclined to believe in their cause because they themselves don't live like they believe in it. The message is only as powerful as those who live it, not by those who believe it.

I'm sick and tired of people who are guilty of lip service. I'm tired of "Christians" who go to church on Sundays and think that is all they need to do. I'm sick of "Christians" who go to church on Sundays and then go to work on Mondays and act like a pagan. I'm tired of "Christians" who bow their heads in prayer during a business lunch meeting and then act unethically after lunch. I'm sick of "Christians" who go to church on Sunday morning and then swear and curse at their basketball game Sunday night. I'm tired of "Christians" who forget that they are playing volleyball in a church league. I'm sick of Christians who go to church on Sunday and then cheat on a test at school on Monday. I'm tired of "Christians" who go to youth group on Wednesday night and then make fun of their classmates at school on Thursday. Quite simply, I'm just sick and tired.

Now, those guilty of following the religion of lip service will likely say that all that is required to become a Christian and get into heaven is that they repent of their sins and accept Jesus as the Christ. I would agree with them. However, I also know that the Bible says that God will demand an accounting of our life when we get into heaven. What will be the impact on those that engage in lip service? Will they be able to go to heaven, even if their faith produced no works? I don't know, but I don't think I want to take the chance and find out when it's too late. No, on second thought, I am sure that I don't want to take the chance. I'll strive to walk the talk today and everyday. How about you?

Somewhere along the way, life got in the way. I started working longer hours in my day job. When I wasn't working, I was stressing about the work that needed to be done. I got involved with the local soccer scene. I spent time creating and strengthening friendships and relationships. I drifted away from our venture, but Dad kept working because he believed in the company's mission. He kept creating content, hoping that I would find time to get back and join him in this all-important mission of reaching out to non-believers. Eventually, after a few years, he reluctantly abandoned ship as well.

The message that I want to convey in this last "Roger's Ramblings" is two-fold. First, whether we are believers or non-believers, we all need to take the letter to Laodicea to heart. Second, and more importantly, I share this story about Dad and his involvement to support me as an example of a Father's love. If my earthly father was that invested in me, how greatly do you think our Heavenly Father is invested in each and every one of us? This is truly what the letter to Laodicea was: A love letter from our loving Father to children that needed loving discipline and encouragement to remember their faith.

Bad Behavior Has Consequences

"I am about to spit you out of my mouth." (Revelation 3:16, NIV)

We apologize in advance for some of the content of this section. But it is necessary to discuss the nature of spewing things out of one's mouth because this is the imagery that Jesus used to describe what will happen to those who are lukewarm. The metaphor of spitting something lukewarm out of the mouth would have resonated with the readers because history tells us that happened when visitors tasted the water in Laodicea. They immediately spit it out because it was lukewarm.

Before we get into specific bodily functions, it is necessary to compare the language in modern translations of the Bible and earlier translations. The New International Version (NIV) is one of the most widely-used modern translations. As you can read above, the NIV translation uses the word "spit". However, earlier translations such as the King James and Amplified Bibles use the word "spew" instead. The New King James version uses the word "vomit". So which version correctly describes the degree of disgust that Jesus has to lukewarm believers? The original Greek word in the original text is "emeo" which is translated to mean "to vomit".

This is one instance where NIV translation probably doesn't do a sufficient job of communicating the intent in the original language of the letter. When Jesus instructed John to write about the consequence of the believers in Laodicea's behavior, He didn't mean it as a simple spit out of the mouth, like we would spit excess saliva or a piece of gum out of our mouth. No, what was intended was a forceful action, something that started in the abdomen and was a thrusting out of the mouth of something that doesn't belong. In this context, vomiting is a better word. When you are feeling ill and the urge to vomit arises, there is nothing you can do to stop the action. It's going to happen. Your body is quite literally rejecting something from it and expelling it, with great force, out of and away from the body.

This is how Jesus felt about the church in Laodicea. Get it out and as soon as possible! Not a good position to be in considering that the goal of the church is to be in fellowship with Jesus.

There's another instance in the above verse where the NIV translation differs from other translations. The earlier translations record that Jesus "will" vomit the church from His mouth, while the NIV says that He is "about to" spit them out of His mouth. A subtle difference, but there is a difference between saying you are about to do something compared to saying that you will do something. For example: there is a difference between saying "I am about to go to work" versus saying "I will go to work". The usage of the word "about to" indicates flexibility and the potential for a possible change. Usage of the word "will" indicates firmness. Using our previous example, when I say that I will go to work, I am committing to going to work, regardless of traffic, car breakdowns, a long line at the coffee shop, etc.

Let's return to the verse and apply what we have learned to it. Jesus was actually saying that "I will remove you from my body forcefully". We can't speak for you, but this seems to be a significant warning of what will happen if we are found to be lukewarm.

Repent! It's Not Too Late!

"I counsel you to buy from me gold refined in the fire, so you can become rich; and white clothes to wear, so you can cover your shameful nakedness; and salve to put on your eyes, so you can see. Those whom I love I rebuke and discipline. So be earnest and repent." (Revelation 3:18-19, NIV)

The imagery in verses 18 and 19 speak directly to the wonderful possibility of redemption. After reading the text of what we call verses 15-17 in the letter, the believers in Laodicea would have been at a low point. So what does Jesus do; does He continue kicking them while they are down? No, quite the opposite actually. He provides a path to returning to their faith.

We are going to go out on a limb and make the following assertion: none of us like to be rebuked or disciplined. When we were children, we would do whatever possible to hide when we hear the words, "wait until your father (or mother) gets home." We knew discipline was coming. It wasn't going to be a fun time; there was going to be a difficult conversation about what we did, why it was wrong, why we did it, what we should have done, and the consequences of our decisions and actions.

We can't speak for you, but we generally deserved the rebukes and consequences. We are glad for it now because it was necessary to improve our character. When done with love, it worked: we learned valuable lessons that strengthened us. We grew when we heard what we didn't want to hear and when we took the message to heart.

What a fantastic couple of verses 18 and 19 are. Literally, immediately after Jesus told the believers that their behavior was so abhorrent that He was going to toss them from the pit of His stomach, He lovingly provided a way back to relationship with Him. Much like a parent rebukes and corrects out of love, Jesus did the same. Let's dive into the path back to relationship that He offered:

- "Buy from me gold refined in the fire" - Like now, gold stands alone amongst the metals because of its ability to withstand impurities. Gold is pure. Jesus was offering the believers a chance to put their impure ways behind them and back into a holy relationship with Him.

- "White clothes to wear" - The message with this phrase is two-fold. First, the offer of clothes was meant to cover their sinful behavior (aka: nakedness). Second, Jesus makes the point that the clothes will be white in color. Previously we explained the importance of the color white and how it symbolized purity in ancient times. Jesus is offering a method to move on from wickedness to the believers.

- "Salve to put on your eyes" - At some point, we all have had a child or pet that has a buildup of gunk around the eyes that was impacting their ability to see adequately. How do we remedy this situation? Through medicine, which clears up the issue and the loved one can see again. This is what Jesus was offering: a chance to come back into relationship with Him and see things clearly. This phrase also related to their advanced eye medicine, showing how He knew them well.

- "Those whom I love I rebuke and discipline" - Jesus didn't hate the believers in Laodicea. Quite the contrary actually. He could have just brushed off His hands and said, "Good riddance. Have a nice life". But He didn't. He wanted them to come back into relationship with Him. He actually wants ALL of us, even today, to enter into relationship with Him.

But, it wasn't going to be easy. Back in the day, a favorite saying was that "backsliding is easy". This is true for believers today and, of course, was true for believers back in John's time. It was going to take work to put their sin behind them and focus on living according to Jesus's calling.

These verses end with that glorious word: "repent". Whatever had happened in their lives previously to this letter, the believers could overcome and move back into a right relationship with Jesus.

Why would they want to repent? For the reward of course.

Answer the Door!
"Here I am! I stand at the door and knock. If anyone hears my voice and opens the door, I will come in and eat with that person, and they with me." (Revelation 3:20, NIV)

Most of us have seen the painting that depicts Jesus standing outside of a door, waiting to be let into the house. The explanation of the painting is that Jesus is wanting us to open the door so that He can come into relationship with us. And this is true. But take a closer look at how the door is depicted in the painting and notice how it is different from doors in our society.

Primarily, there were no handles or door knobs on the outside of doors in ancient times. Doors were meant for a purpose: to keep people out. Unless the person on the outside was permitted entrance by the person inside, they were not allowed entrance. Doors today have handles or knobs on both sides of the door. The lock on the door is the mechanism to prevent a person from gaining entrance to the inside of the house or building. Think back to the movies about medieval times when an army tried to conquer a castle. The only way they could get into the castle was to knock the door down with a battering ram.

The implication to this passage is that Jesus cannot gain entrance to our hearts and lives unless we open the door. There aren't any handles or knobs that He will use to force Himself into our hearts. He's not going to knock down the doors. Only we can open the door to Him.

When the believers in Laodicea opened the door and let Jesus into their hearts, they were promised to be able to share dinner with Jesus. In other words, they were able to fellowship with Him. We have that same promise today, but first, we must open the door.

As a corollary to this text: To whom do you need to open the door to in your life? There is an old saying in the sales field that goes like this: "What is the hardest door to open when you are a salesperson? The car door." The car door isn't going to open itself; it takes effort on the salesperson to go out and get to work. There is an analogy in this saying to thriving amidst the chaos. How can you repair that relationship with friend or family member that has been fractured for years? Open the door. In other words, make the phone call. Send the text message. Mail a greeting card. Relationship restoration is important for our lives. Oftentimes you have to take the first step.

Hmmm. Relationship restoration. That's a good lesson from the picture of Jesus knocking at the door. He longs to restore a relationship with us. Let's follow His example and restore our relationships.

The Ultimate Reward

"To the one who is victorious, I will give the right to sit with me on my throne, just as I was victorious and sat down with my Father on his throne." (Revelation 3:21, NIV)

As we wrap up this book, we are struck by the impact of reward possible for the Laodiceans. The title to this section says it all: the ultimate reward. The implication from this text reflects the glorious reward awaiting those going to heaven because they have a relationship with Jesus. Imagine sitting on a throne in the presence of God and Jesus forever. For. Ever. If you think waiting in line at the DMV takes forever, you haven't seen anything yet. This is the pinnacle of all possible rewards that we can enjoy in this life. Cash money, a big house, a shiny sports car, or a personal jet, all pale compared to reigning with God in heaven for all eternity.

But there is another reward for believers that is nearly as good. That reward is seeing non-believers coming to faith in Jesus and creating their own relationship with Him. Especially if those non-believers happen to be close friends or family. Nothing is harder for a believer than to attend a funeral of such a person when they were taken from this Earth before they were able to enter into this relationship. Remember the process outlined in this letter: "You've been bad, but if you repent, you can join me (Jesus) in heaven forever". How we wish all of our friends, family members, and close acquaintances would follow this process. (Actually, we wish all people everywhere would follow this process.)

Did you notice the tie-in between the ultimate reward and thriving amidst chaos? It's related to the above paragraph. Improving the lives of others has a direct impact on our ability to thrive amidst chaos. What better improvement to someone else's life could there be than to show God to them through your example? When they make course corrections in their lives and start getting closer to God, the intended consequence for your life is that you start to thrive.

Although this verse is primarily for believers, making a positive impact on the lives of others has relevance for non-believers as well. Even if your light doesn't align with God, you can still make a positive impact on those around you and alter their current situation. You will stop focusing on your problems and begin to thrive amidst the chaos of our society.

For the Last Time: Pay Attention

"Whoever has ears, let them hear what the Spirit says to the churches" *(Revelation 3:22, NIV)*

As we noted earlier in this chapter, the history seems to indicate that the Laodiceans actually *did* listen and pay attention to what the letter to their church said. The believers took the rebuke and discipline, changed their lives, and grew in their faith.

The lesson for us is obvious: we need to turn away from our wicked ways, repent, and live for Jesus in order to receive the ultimate reward.

The question for you is also obvious: What's stopping you from making this course correction today?

Points to Ponder with Jeff: Accept What He Offers

Over the last several years something has happened in the church world that is an interesting phenomena – I call it "church shopping". People want to find a church that fits their wants and desires and that they feel comfortable in. I am not saying that is wrong. I understand that. But what is interesting is what their "shopping list" seem to contain:

- Size of church (large, small, just right)
- Worship style (Loud or soft music, hymns or contemporary, instruments)
- Preacher (Skill, attire, preaching style, personal style)
- Church facilities (Pew comfort, parking lot experience)

I don't know if you realized it or not, none of the things that were included in the survey ever came from the mouth of Jesus as He addressed His church in Revelation. But I'm pretty sure I have heard some of those things from the mouths of people in my 45 years of ministry experience who were looking for a church.

Today we are looking at Jesus's words to the church of Laodicea. They are considered by many as the harshest words Jesus gave to any of the seven churches. I want us to hear the message of Jesus and understand it – not just what it meant to the churches of Asia Minor – but what it means to us.

Warning #1: Accept the truth of His words

Review the credentials given by Jesus in verses 14-16. Jesus uses the phrase "the Amen" to denote that He was (is) the one who is affirmed by God. His use of the phrase "the faithful and true witness" speaks to how He is reliable. When Jesus refers to the "rule of God's creation", it means that He is authoritative.

We need to accept His words as they are: truth. Even if sometimes they make us uncomfortable. When Jesus is in the midst of His church He looks at more than the sanctuary or building. He looks at the heart of its people and He wants their heart to be in the right place. He wants to have priority. If I told my wife that when it came to women, she was in the top 5, how do you think that would go over? Let me assure you that it would not go very well. Why? Because she is to be number 1. And of course she is.

Jesus wants to be number 1 but His illustration of being lukewarm is very vivid and easy to understand to the people then and to us now. Jesus's reference to the lukewarm water hit home with the Laodiceans. Everyone hearing the words of Jesus would have immediately known what He was referring to.

What had made them lukewarm? I think we will find as we read on that what brought their lukewarmness was self-sufficiency. When we become self-sufficient it becomes easier and easier to forget about God.

What about the usage of the words hot or cold; what does it mean? Sometimes we hear this passage and think that it means to be "hot" we are "on fire"" for Jesus and to be "cold" means we reject Him. But that interpretation doesn't make sense because it would mean Jesus is saying He would rather someone reject Him; to be "cold" rather than anything else. He desires that everyone accept Him.

Think of it this way: cold water is what most people desire. It is cool and refreshing. Just as hot water is what you want when you have coffee or tea. Both are desirable and both are good. But when was the last time you asked for lukewarm water or lukewarm coffee. That is not desirable.

Jesus's words of truth are simply this: He wants us to take our faith serious. He wants our faith to make faith desirable to others. If our faith does not lead others to Jesus, then we are missing the mark that He wants us to hit.

Warning #2: Accept His wise counsel

Jesus's words in verses 17-18 once again directly connected to the people who lived in Laodicea. What did Jesus say to them? He uses quite direct words: "you are wretched, pitiful, poor, blind and naked". What is the remedy? How do you overcome all of that? First, Accept His counsel. Second, we are to turn to Him rather than ourselves. Thirdly, get your "gold", the symbol of wealth, not from yourself. What Jesus has is worth much more than gold. Fourth, if you want clothing that will truly impress people, clothe yourself with Christ – put on a white robe representing holiness and eternal life. Finally, you want to see, really see? Apply what Jesus has to offer in your life.

What I have just said is more than just cliches. It is truth. I don't feel I can adequately express what I am feeling. I have seen so many lives ruined by people who were seeking meaning or fulfillment in their life through alcohol or drugs or sex or fame or power or prestige – people searching and looking everywhere except Jesus. The life Jesus offers is right in front of us if we will just accept the blessings we have.

Warning #3: Accept His loving rebuke

Did you ever use this line when you were disciplining your kids – "This is going to hurt me more than it hurts you." As a kid, how many of you believed that line? But as a parent you have a different perspective don't you? The purpose of discipline is to give direction. To help someone realize what is harmful or wrong and making a correction.

What does Jesus want? He desires that all people be saved. For that to happen sometimes we have to accept a loving rebuke. This is what He is doing in verse 19.

One of the challenges of preaching the word of God in today's world is that people are going to hear things that they don't agree with. Rather than accept those words as words of loving rebuke, they often take offense and reject God's way.

Warning #4: Accept His invitation and promises

Sometimes our understanding of various imagery used in the Bible is affected by the progression of our society throughout time. When we think of a door, what comes to mind is a structure, often wood, that has a handle on both the outside and the inside. But in the times when John wrote this letter, doors largely did not contain a handle on the outside and could only be opened from the inside.

The imagery Jesus uses in this letter to the church of Laodicea is sad. He feels He is not a part of the church. He is offering Himself when He said, "Here I am!" He is standing at the door and knocking, hoping that someone will let Him in.

I wonder how many thousands and thousands of people over the years heard Jesus knocking on their hearts but never opened the door. I remember as a teenager going to youth rallies and seeing hundreds of teens not respond to the messages that were calling people to come into a relationship with Jesus.

Warning #5: Accept His challenge

It is not enough to simply read about Jesus. We must accept Him as our Lord and Savior.

Today, let us not be lukewarm.

Dig Deeper: Questions to Consider from Chapter 3

There were three very different churches covered in the third chapter of Revelation. First, we discussed Sardis, the dead church. Then John's writing does a complete 180 degree change and includes the letter to the church in Philadelphia, the "good" church. Finally, the chapter ends with the letter to the church in Laodicea, which was a lesson in redemption.

Did you find yourself in one of the letters to these three churches? If you are a believer or a regular church attender, did you find your church in one of these letters? No? Well, let's dive deeper.

1. When was the last time that you had a performance review at work where you went in thinking that you were great but it became immediately obvious that your supervisor disagreed? Perhaps they even thought the exact opposite. Why the disconnect? Was it on your end or theirs? We assume that this happens to everyone at some point in their lives. Why are we sometimes unable to accurately assess our behavior, thoughts, and actions? How can we overcome this personal blindness?

2. Staying in reference to Sardis, take a minute and conduct a mental evaluation of the level at which you reach out to others and help them in their life's journey. Remember that focusing on others is one of the important aspects of thriving amidst the chaos. Where can you improve? What steps will you take today to improve?

3. Moving on to Philadelphia. There is a focus in the letter on the benefits of endurance in our relationship with Jesus. This also applies to our daily lives as well. Where in your life can you improve your endurance? We'll provide an example. There is a co-worker that constantly gives you the cold shoulder. They don't acknowledge when you say, "Good morning". They just grunt when you try to talk to them. When can you stop trying and just start ignoring them. Answer? Never. You need to endure and keep reaching out.

4. Name your favorite lukewarm food item, other than pizza leftover from last night. How about French fries? Do you like them hot or lukewarm? Time for an honest assessment. Where in your life are you lukewarm in your relationships with others? Why? What are some steps that you can do today to get rid of lukewarmness?

5. Are you a good listener? What would others say, including your spouse or significant other? Would they agree or would they say that you need some work listening? After reading chapter three in the book of Revelation, did you read and listen or did you just skim through it? How can you demonstrate that you've listened to the content and messages of chapter three in your life today?

PART FIVE

AFTERWORD

Epilogue

Well, that's a wrap for this book. All of these pages in our book and we are just through the first three chapters of the book of Revelation. Some have suggested that it would be better to just write one book, but as you have discovered, the amount of content in Revelation is too great.

So the story is not finished. Our analysis of how the book of Revelation can help us thrive in our daily lives will continue in the near future. You will want to join us as we discover what God is telling us when John writes about the throne room of God, the battle between good and evil, and what heaven is going to resemble.

Thank you for joining us on this journey. We invite you to join us on those journeys as well.

Revelation: A Challenging Read

Congratulations! You've made it through the first three chapters of Revelation. By now, you've come to realize that Revelation is challenging to read, comprehend, and understand. But only by studying will you gain an appreciation for God's power and plan over the evil that satan brought into the world. At times you may be frustrated because you don't understand the meaning behind the sixth trumpet blast. But don't dismay: the topics covered in this book series will allow you to suspend that frustration because we focus on the ultimate meaning behind all the trumpet blasts in relation to heaven and eternal life.

So make sure your seat is upright, your tray tables are locked in the upright position, and that your seat belt is firmly secure. We're in for a ride together!

Dig Deeper: Questions to Consider from Chapters 2 & 3

As we conclude this study of the letters to the seven churches, we feel that it is appropriate to have a final chance at digging deeper into the Scripture in order to apply it to your life.

At the beginning of the section about the letters to the seven churches, we discussed how the structure of the letters was similar:

There is a description of Jesus that establishes Him as the ultimate author of the letter, there are praises for good work, some things that need to be worked on, a call to repentance, and a reward for those that stand firm in the faith.

1. What are some of the good things you've accomplished in your life? Easy there; don't break your arm patting yourself on the back. Just provide an honest account.

2. What do you need to work on?

3. God calls us to repent. How do you recognize your need to repent?

4. What excites you most about the reward?

5. "He who has an ear..." What are 3-5 concrete actions that you can take in your life to demonstrate that you've taken chapters 2 & 3 to heart?

———————————————————————

Personal Note (Roger)

When Jeff announced in the beginning of 2023 that he was going to be preaching a series on the book of Revelation, my brain went into overdrive. I had recently finished the second book in the Thriving Amidst Adversity series and was pulling together content for the third and final book in that series. But I couldn't get away from the thought of taking Jeff's life-long learning journey about Revelation and making it available to the public in written form. At the same time, the outside world seemed to be getting more and more challenging for people to navigate successfully. We thought that life would get back to normal after the Covid-19 period concluded. But the stress in our lives from Covid was only replaced with stress from an economic downturn that the television news media kept telling us was just around the corner. Then in the midst of all that, countries around the world are fighting and threatening to bring the world to the brink of global warfare. Not to mention all of the weather-related disasters occurring simultaneously.

Stress is nothing new. Our parents were stressed about nuclear war. Their parents were stressed during the Great Depression. Their parents were stressed about the "war to end all wars", which actually wasn't the first of those. But for us, it seems different. The challenges and pressures facing our society seem more extreme.

This backstop was in my mind as I read through Jeff's sermon schedule and preliminary outline. I then turned to the text of Revelation and did some reading. They all seemed to be aligning at a central focal point: What if you worked with Jeff to create a book that would glean application from the book of Revelation for people's daily lives? This confluence seemed to be Him speaking as to the need for this message to our society today.

So I took Jeff out for lunch one day and explained my crazy idea. And to my surprise, he didn't say no! He agreed that the idea had promise. As a pastor of a church, he is extremely busy so I sold him on the idea that all I needed from him was to act as a "spiritual consultant". He would read my content and comment on whether it was accurate from a scriptural standpoint. That was my hook to get him to agree. I have been delighted that his participation has exceeded my expectations because he brings a lot of strengths to the writing process. If you were to go back and read this book with a discerning eye, it will become immediately obvious which sections are his because they are written tremendously better than my sections.

Speaking of writing, this book surprised me because it took a long time to write. As soon as I finished one section and tried to move on to the next passage of scripture, I'd have an inspirational thought about a previous section. The text was so strong that I kept finding additional things to say about every passage.

I hope you are looking forward to the next book as much as I am.

Personal Note (Jeff)

Although I have written many sermons and many papers in college and graduate school, this is the first time I have tried to collect my thoughts in a book. It is something I have thought about in the past but had never done. The one prayer I have for this book, as with all my sermons, is "Lord, help me to accurately communicate your Word to others". Hopefully you gain a better understanding of what God has to say to you in the Book of Revelation.

Acknowledgments

We both would like to express our gratitude for everyone in our lives that made this journey possible.

We would like to thank everyone that read some portion of the manuscript and provided comment. Your participation in this editing process strengthened the book and resulted in a stronger end product. Thank you Betty N, Donna V, Tim L, and Mary Lou A!

Jeff would like to thank Roger for asking him to be a part of this project; he has put a lot of work in bringing all of this together. I must also thank all my professors at Lincoln Christian College and Seminary who taught me the skills needed for studying and communicating God's Word. Finally, I must say thank you to my wife Judy. She has been my encouragement and partner in the Gospel from the very beginning.

Roger would like to thank the friends and family members who continued to push to make this project a reality. Life got in the way several times during the writing and this book easily could have been abandoned and placed on a shelf had it not been for hearing from people "how's the book coming? I'm looking forward to reading it!". Thank you all; I hope it's been worth the wait! Last but certainly not least, this project was blessed to have been reviewed by Donna H. Despite our back-and-forth regarding the copious amounts of red ink on the manuscript, your input made the book infinitely better than the first draft. Thank you. Your editing and patience are greatly appreciated!

PART SIX

BONUS SECTION: PLAN OF SALVATION

Points to Ponder with Jeff: God's Plan of Salvation

"To him who loves us and has freed us from our sins by his blood and has made us to be a kingdom and priests to serve his God and Father" (Revelation 1:5-6, NIV)

Speaking of Jesus as the faithful witness, we would be remiss if we did not present God's plan of salvation somewhere in this book. The following is a scripture study lesson from Jeff on God's plan of salvation.

First, we need to start with a basic question. What does the Bible teach about God's plan of salvation? It sounds like a simple question but it is amazing all the different answers that have been derived over the years. I want to try and answer that question as simply as I know how. I want to tell you my approach to this topic. I tried to set aside all the "plans of salvation" that I had heard over the years. Put away the workbooks on becoming a Christian. Didn't look at the many tracts that are available on the subject. Here's what I did. I typed in the word "save" and did a concordance search of the New Testament. I looked at all the verses that directly mentioned what man needs to do to be saved. You know what? It was a fascinating study. Because what I found is more complete than all the notebooks or gospel tracts that I've ever read. Imagine that, finding God's plan for saving mankind spelled out simply in His Word. What a concept!

So, what I am going to share with you is the result of that study. I am briefly going to share with you the nine things I found in scripture that specifically mentions what we need to do and what happens when a person is saved. I believe that all nine are essential. We do not have the right to pick and choose from the list the one's we like or the one's we are the most comfortable with. This is how we have come up with so many different views of what it takes to find salvation in Jesus Christ. One group has taken this verse and built their salvation theology around it, another group has taken one or two other verses and built their salvation theology around them, etc. Who do we think we are to be able to pick and choose the verses we like most. God's word is complete and whole and we need to take His Word as a whole.

For the remainder of this section, I am going to briefly touch on all these passages with the conviction that all of them are important and essential if we want to follow God's plan of salvation.

Step 1: You must hear the message of Christ

Hearing the message of Christ is the first basic step. The power of the spoken word is something never to be underestimated. The course of history has been changed many times by the power of the spoken word. Speeches have been given that have inspired nations to war. Some of you today could tell us exactly what you were doing when you heard famous speeches. It is rather hard to act upon something without actually hearing a compelling message first. So it is with the Gospel and the process of becoming saved. Consider the following passages that speak to the importance of hearing Christ's message:

"Where is the wise man? Where is the scholar? Where is the philosopher of this age? Has not God made foolish the wisdom of the world? For since in the wisdom of God the world through its wisdom did not know him, God was pleased through the foolishness of what was preached to save those who believe." (1 Corinthians 1:20-21, NIV)

"Now, brothers, I want to remind you of the gospel I preached to you, which you received and on which you have taken your stand. By this gospel you are saved, if you hold firmly to the word I preached to you. Otherwise, you have believed in vain. For what I received I passed on to you as of first importance: that Christ died for our sins according to the Scriptures, that he was buried, that he was raised on the third day according to the Scriptures." (1 Corinthians 15:1-4, NIV)

"How, then, can they call on the one they have not believed in? And how can they believe in the one of whom they have not heard? And how can they hear without someone preaching to them?" (Romans 10:14, NIV)

Step 2: You must believe in Jesus Christ, the Son of God

Once you have heard the message, the next step is to believe that Jesus is the Son of God. The same Jesus to whom the book of Revelation is written about. Consider these passages that speak to the importance of believing in Jesus:

"For God so loved the world that he gave his one and only Son, that whoever believes in him shall not perish but have eternal life. For God did not send his Son

into the world to condemn the world, but to save the world through him."
(John 3:16-17, NIV)

"Suddenly there was such a violent earthquake that the foundations of the prison were shaken. At once all the prison doors flew open, and everybody's chains came loose. The jailer woke up, and when he saw the prison doors open, he drew his sword and was about to kill himself because he thought the prisoners had escaped. But Paul shouted, 'Don't harm yourself! We are all here!' The jailer called for lights, rushed in and fell trembling before Paul and Silas. He then brought them out and asked, 'Sirs, what must I do to be saved?' They replied, 'Believe in the Lord Jesus, and you will be saved-- you and your household.' Then they spoke the word of the Lord to him and to all the others in his house. At that hour of the night the jailer took them and washed their wounds; then immediately he and all his family were baptized." (Acts 16:26-33, NIV)

Step 3: You must call on the Lord

Becoming a Christian means that God will apply mercy and grace to us so that we can escape the result of our sinful nature. But in order to receive His mercy and grace, we must first ask Him. We cannot rely on ourselves. Consider the following passages:

"'And everyone who calls on the name of the Lord will be saved.' 'Men of Israel, listen to this: Jesus of Nazareth was a man accredited by God to you by miracles, wonders and signs, which God did among you through him, as you yourselves know. This man was handed over to you by God's set purpose and foreknowledge; and you, with the help of wicked men, put him to death by nailing him to the cross. But God raised him from the dead, freeing him from the agony of death, because it was impossible for death to keep its hold on him.'" (Acts 2:21-24, NIV)

"Salvation is found in no one else, for there is no other name under heaven given to men by which we must be saved." (Acts 4:12, NIV)

Step 4: You must repent of your sins

When we call on God, the intent of our conversation is to wipe our slate clean. Which He is willing to do, but we must ask for forgiveness. And not just ask for forgiveness, but genuinely repent of our evil self. Consider the following passage:

"'Therefore let all Israel be assured of this: God has made this Jesus, whom you crucified, both Lord and Christ.' When the people heard this, they were cut to the heart and said to Peter and the other apostles, 'Brothers, what shall we do?' Peter replied, 'Repent and be baptized, every one of you, in the name of Jesus Christ for the forgiveness of your sins. And you will receive the gift of the Holy Spirit.'" (Acts 2:36-38, NIV)

Step 5: You must confess that Jesus is Lord

The next step is to confess to God that you believe that Jesus is Lord of your life. The mercy and grace that you have received compel you to put those evil ways behind and let the love of Jesus rule in your heart. Consider the following passage:

"That if you confess with your mouth, 'Jesus is Lord,' and believe in your heart that God raised him from the dead, you will be saved. For it is with your heart that you believe and are justified, and it is with your mouth that you confess and are saved. As the Scripture says, 'Anyone who trusts in him will never be put to shame.'" (Romans 10:9-13, NIV)

Step 6: You must be baptized

The Bible is clear that baptism is a crucial component of the path to salvation. There are numerous links between the act of baptism and the resultant act of salvation. Consider the following passages:

"He said to them, 'Go into all the world and preach the good news to all creation. Whoever believes and is baptized will be saved, but whoever does not believe will be condemned.'" (Mark 16:15-16, NIV)

"For Christ died for sins once for all, the righteous for the unrighteous, to bring you to God. He was put to death in the body but made alive by the Spirit, through whom also he went and preached to the spirits in prison who disobeyed long ago when God waited patiently in the days of Noah while the ark was being built. In it only a few people, eight in all, were saved through water, and this water symbolizes baptism that now saves you also-- not the removal of dirt from the body but the pledge of a good conscience toward God. It saves you by the resurrection of Jesus Christ" (1 Peter 3:18-22, NIV)

"'Therefore let all Israel be assured of this: God has made this Jesus, whom you crucified, both Lord and Christ.' When the people heard this, they were cut to the heart and said to Peter and the other apostles, 'Brothers, what shall we do?' Peter replied, 'Repent and be baptized, every one of you, in the name of Jesus Christ for the forgiveness of your sins. And you will receive the gift of the Holy Spirit.'" (Acts 2:36-38, NIV)

Step 7: You must be sanctified through the Holy Spirit

The definition of "sanctification" is: consecration, purification, the effect of consecration, the cleaning of the heart and life. Once you are on the path of salvation that will ultimately lead to heaven, you must get rid of your old self. The following passages speak to this importance:

"But we ought always to thank God for you, brothers loved by the Lord, because from the beginning God chose you to be saved through the sanctifying work of the Spirit and through belief in the truth. He called you to this through our gospel, that you might share in the glory of our Lord Jesus Christ." (2 Thessalonians 2:13, NIV)

"At one time we too were foolish, disobedient, deceived and enslaved by all kinds of passions and pleasures. We lived in malice and envy, being hated and hating one another. But when the kindness and love of God our Savior appeared, he saved us, not because of righteous things we had done, but because of his mercy. He saved us through the washing of rebirth and renewal by the Holy Spirit, whom he poured out on us generously through Jesus Christ our Savior, so that, having been justified by his grace, we might become heirs having the hope of eternal life." (Titus 3:3-7, NIV)

Step 8: You must receive God's gift of saving grace

The definition of God's saving grace is: good will, loving-kindness, favor; used of the merciful kindness by which God, exerting His holy influence upon souls, turns them to Christ, keeps, strengthens, increases them in Christian faith, knowledge, affection, and kindles them to the exercise of the Christian virtues. Consider the following passage:

"As for you, you were dead in your transgressions and sins, in which you used to live when you followed the ways of this world and of the ruler of the kingdom of the air, the spirit who is now at work in those who are disobedient. All of us also lived among them at one time, gratifying the cravings of our sinful nature and following its desires and thoughts. Like the rest, we were by nature objects of wrath. But because of his great love for us, God, who is rich in mercy, made us alive with Christ even when we were dead in transgressions-it is by grace you have been saved. And God raised us up with Christ and seated us with him in the heavenly realms in Christ Jesus, in order that in the coming ages he might show the incomparable riches of his grace, expressed in his kindness to us in Christ Jesus. For it is by grace you have been saved, through faith-and this not from yourselves, it is the gift of God-not by works, so that no one can boast." (Ephesians 2:1-9, NIV)

Step 9: You must live a consistent Christian life

Quite simply, live a life that demonstrates your commitment to the new life rather than your old sinful life. Consider the following passages:

"Therefore, get rid of all moral filth and the evil that is so prevalent and humbly accept the word planted in you, which can save you. Do not merely listen to the word, and so deceive yourselves. Do what it says." (James 1:21-22, NIV)

"Be diligent in these matters; give yourself wholly to them, so that everyone may see your progress. Watch your life and doctrine closely. Persevere in them, because if you do, you will save both yourself and your hearers." (1 Timothy 4:15-16, NIV)

PART SEVEN

BONUS SECTION: OVERVIEW OF REVELATION

Want to Learn More?

When we started writing this book, we realized that it would immediately resonate with believers and followers of Christ - Jesus's message for the early believers also apply to us some two-thousand years later. However, as we progressed into the text of Revelation, it quickly became apparent that this book also had application to those who do not subscribe to Christianity, go to church, etc.

This section of the book is intended to create an appreciation for continued study of the book of Revelation. Now that you've read and studied the first three chapters, you might as well continue on with chapter 4 and so on, at least until our next book is released. This is true for both the non-believer and for the believer who has never studied the book of Revelation.

The Author

"John, To the seven churches in the province of Asia." (Revelation 1:4, NIV)

Introduction

This section is a bit lengthy, but stay with us as it is important to fully understand the person who wrote the book of Revelation. He wasn't a super hero or "super-Christian", simply just a human being, the same as all of us reading this book. The difference is how he lived his life and what he accomplished in life as the result of walking and talking with Jesus and being open to His message of hope.

Too often this world brings us down and we feel like we'll never amount to anything worthwhile, the opposite of thriving. Most of us won't have a prominent role in society like the author of Revelation had, but we have an important role in the lives of those around us. We are all ordinary. But let's investigate the author's life to discover how we can help others thrive.

His Name was John

Before we begin, we will conduct an experiment. Grab a pen and a piece of scrap paper and write down all the people that you know that have been given the name "John". How many can you think of within a minute or two? How many "John's" do you know?

The purpose of this exercise is to demonstrate that throughout history, the name John has been very important. Pope John Paul. John Kennedy. King John. John Elway. John Wesley. There have literally been thousands, if not millions, of people named John since time has been recorded and in many cultures - Spanish ("Juan"), French ("John"), German ("John"), etc. Even within the Bible, there were multiple people with the name "John": John the Baptist, the apostle John, and others. So who was the man named John that wrote the book of Revelation?

John's Background

John, the author of Revelation, was a close follower of Jesus, commonly called an "apostle" or "disciple". He was not John the Baptist. This is the John that not only wrote the book of Revelation, but also wrote the book Gospel of John as well as three additional letters to early churches that are included in the New Testament. But more on these later.

We first read of John in the book of Matthew: "Going on from there, he [Jesus] saw two other brothers, James son of Zebedee and his brother John. They were in a boat with their father Zebedee, preparing their nets. Jesus called them, and immediately they left the boat and their father and followed him." (Matthew 4:21-22, NIV). A similar story is recorded in the gospel of Mark.

From these short passages of scripture, we know the following about John:

- His father's name was Zebedee but we actually don't know anything about Zebedee, either in the written Bible or through the oral tradition.
- His brother's name was James, who also became a disciple of Jesus.
- The family were fishermen, typical work in that time. If a family lived near the water, they would have worked the boats to catch fish to eat and sell. John's life would have been hard, waking up early to prepare the boats and equipment with long hours on the water. More than once the Bible mentions that fishermen were working through the night to catch their quota of fish.

- John immediately left behind the boat, his career as a fisherman, and his family to follow Jesus. It is quite possible that once John left the boat, he may not have seen his family again.

It is easy for us today to cast dispersions on John and James for leaving their family and work behind to follow someone that was preaching a message that seemed weird to the public. But it was precisely this new message of hope that attracted them to follow Jesus. Their lives before Jesus showed up were marked by the opposite of hope: they were destined to a life of drudgery and hard work for little pay. Jesus offered them hope if they left the "security" of this world to cleave to the "certainty" of the next world. As they walked besides Jesus during His ministry, it is no surprise that they were devoted.

<u>John the Disciple</u>
The Bible tells us that there were twelve men that were considered Jesus's disciples. These men were all personally called to the ministry by Jesus and they spent the bulk of three years following Jesus. Throughout history, these men have been called "disciples" and "apostles". As we continue our analysis and appreciation of John's background, it is important to understand the difference between those two words. First, we will analyze the word "disciple".

The Greek word that is used is "mathetes", which literally means "a learner". The depth of the Greek word is deeper than our definition - when we think of a learner, we think of the student in elementary school, high school, or higher eduction such as college. But in the Greek, a disciple was more than just a pupil; the disciple was an imitator of their teacher.

Using this definition, was John a disciple of Jesus? Was he someone who learned from Jesus? Was he an imitator of Jesus? The answer to these questions is a resounding, "Yes". John was a disciple of Jesus.

The importance for us as we find hope in the book of Revelation is that its author (John) had spent many days, weeks, and months directly in the company of Jesus.

John the Apostle

Not only was John a disciple of Jesus, he was also considered an apostle of Jesus. The Greek word that is used in the New Testament is "apostolos" which is defined as a "delegate; specially, an ambassador of the Gospel; officially a commissioner of Christ" (Vine's Expository Dictionary of Biblical Words). The King James applies the concept of being a messenger, one who is sent forth to proclaim the message of Christ.

Was John someone sent on a mission to preach the gospel of Christ? Yes. John was both a disciple of Jesus and an apostle of Jesus.

Sometimes the words apostle and disciple are used synonymously to describe the early followers of Jesus such as John. But the strict definition of the words speak to their differences. A "disciple" is one who follows someone while an "apostle" is someone who goes out to spread the message of that person. The difference is subtle, but profound when we consider the foundation of the book of Revelation. John was a close follower of Jesus, but he was also a major character in the formation of the early church as described in the book of Acts.

John's involvement in the formation of the early church is important to our study of the impact of Revelation on our life because it authenticates John's future writings. John wasn't a disciple who went into hiding after Jesus returned to heaven. No, he was active in promoting the faith and the new message of the importance of accepting Jesus. He devoted his entire life to spreading the good news.

John the Beloved

As we continue building John's story, there is an interesting passage that we must dissect because it helps in our understanding of John. The Gospel of Mark 10:35-45 describes a conversation between James, John, and Jesus regarding their position of authority in Jesus's kingdom. James and John had an interesting request: they wanted to be elevated to the right and left hand of Jesus.

Looking back, we would view this as a clear "what were they thinking" moment. There are a couple of possibilities as to what they might have been thinking. The first possibility is that the two of them were egomaniacs and viewed themselves as closer to Jesus than the other disciples because elsewhere in the New Testament John is described as the one "whom Jesus loved". The fact that this phrase is only found in the Gospel of John (John 13:23, John 19:26, John 21:7, and John 21:20) doesn't bode too well because John uses the phrase to describe himself. Perhaps John did believe himself to be better than the other disciples, yet as we will read later, John's ministry career seemed to indicate that he was a humble leader of the early church. Another possibility is one of ignorance. Before Jesus's birth, the people had interpreted Old Testament prophecy that the Messiah was going to be a great military leader who would free them from the bondage of the Roman Empire. As John and James traveled with Jesus, they no doubt came to the realization that He was the Messiah foretold by the prophets. Their request to be at Jesus's right and left hand might have simply been made by two brothers who thought they were close to a man who would free the people and be set up as king.

Regardless of their intent, Jesus was gracious in his response to their request because he knew that these brothers didn't understand what they were asking. In Mark 10:38-40, Jesus tells them that He is not able to grant their request. Jesus was patient with them because he knew that a military revolution was not going to be waged with the Romans to set up his kingdom on earth. But, the other disciples did not possess the same understanding as Jesus and were angry as described in Mark 10:41-45. This request made by John and James had the potential to negatively impact the new ministry because it generated jealousy and anger. But Jesus turned it into a teaching moment by introducing the concept that their lives would be marked with humility and serving others rather than seeking power.

John the Guardian

"Near the cross of Jesus stood his mother, his mother's sister, Mary the wife of Clopas, and Mary Magdalene. When Jesus saw his mother there, and the disciple whom he loved standing nearby, he said to her, 'Woman, here is your son,' and to the disciple, 'Here is your mother.' From that time on, this disciple took her into his home." (John 19:25-27, NIV)

Wow. What a heavy responsibility was thrust upon John during Jesus's last minutes on earth. Have you ever considered exactly what Jesus was asking of John with this request? This interchange had long lasting effects for all three parties:

- Jesus: In the midst of great suffering and agony, Jesus made sure that his mother was going to be taken care of after he passed from this earth. Equally fully human and fully God, this would have created a sense of peace within his humanness that his mother would not suffer the life of an elderly widow. Jesus also reinforced the foundation of the Old Testament commandment to honor our father and mother.
- Mary: Tradition at that time was that people married young so Mary became Jesus's mother while yet a teenager. Tradition further states that Jesus died around 33 years of age. Simple math tells us that Mary was probably in her late 40's and likely a widow at the time when John assumed responsibility to take care of her. So he likely took care of her for many years, which falls in line with Scripture.
- John: As we will see in the next sections, this request likely impacted John's ministry because he had to remain local to take care of Mary.

John the Evangelist

Curiously, the last mention of John is in chapter 10 of Acts. After that chapter, we do not hear of him until his first letter to a group of churches, the book of 1 John. It is reasonable to assume that John continued spreading the message of Jesus throughout the region and this lack of inclusion in the written record of the early church (IE: The New Testament) doesn't mean that he wasn't active.

Historians say that John spent a decade or so in the region in and around Jerusalem after Jesus returned to heaven. This would have been approximately the time between 33 AD and 45 AD. John would have been working to create new churches as well as strengthening existing churches at the same time.

As the new ministry grew and churches were created, the geopolitical environment quickly became oppressive. Persecution of early believers was always present, but really caught traction during the reign of Herod Agrippa from 41-44 AD. It is during this time that John likely left Jerusalem and went to other parts of the world in an attempt to escape the persecution.

John the Persecuted

Mistreating the early Christians was so rampant in early history that the Romans even utilized the great Colosseum building to use as a venue. A quick search on-line will result in numerous articles describing persecution under Roman emperors such as Nero and will illuminate the extent to which the Romans tried to quell the early church.

Prior to his exile, John was brought to Rome to be persecuted in front of a large audience at the Colosseum to be plunged into a pool of burning oil. But a miracle happened and John emerged from the pool with nary a scratch and as a result of that miracle, many in the audience converted to Christianity.

After the failed attempt to kill John, he ended up in Ephesus, where he wrote the three letters to the early church. John was one who truly understood persecution and suffering. Is it any wonder that he was chosen by God to share the message of Revelation?

John the Author

Besides the book of Revelation, John is credited with writing four other books of the Bible: The gospel of John, 1st John, 2nd John, and 3rd John. The exact location where John wrote these books is unknown, but these books were written later in John's life (50AD+). The gospel of John is his retelling of the life and ministry of Jesus, whereas the books 1st, 2nd, and 3rd John are letters to early churches. Each of these books focused on a different audience and aspect of the early Christian faith. As we continue to learn more about the foundation of the book of Revelation, it is important to know that John was instrumental in both telling about Jesus's ministry on earth (Gospel of John) and His power from Heaven (1st, 2nd, and 3rd John).

The apostle John lived a long life, devoted to following Christ. He lived in the presence of the greatest man in history. He was instrumental laying the foundation for Christianity, the faith that changed the lives of thousands of people at the time (and billions more since). For that he was persecuted relentlessly, quite often to physical harm and the threat of death. But were all these qualifications enough to include his writings in the Bible? Why were his account of the life of Jesus, his letters to the early churches, and his book describing his vision of the end times included in the Bible?

Throughout history, scholars have generally used four criteria factors when deciding which historical writings to include in the Bible:

1. Was the author an apostle or did he have the support of an apostle? Or put another way, did he actually spend time in the presence of Jesus?
2. Did the apostles as a group endorse the writing? The earliest collection of books that we consider the New Testament were evaluated when apostles were still alive.
3. Was the writing circulated among the early churches? In other words, was the accuracy of the writings maintained when they were copied and sent to multiple churches throughout many years and decades?
4. Were the writings immediately and universally accepted by the early church?

John and his writings pass all the criteria so it is important that his foundational writings are included in the New Testament section of the Bible. The book of Revelation is not just a random letter from some random guy in history, it has passed all the tests, and is relevant to our times today.

John the Exiled

The Roman Emperor Domitian faced a difficult situation when the followers of Christ from Palestine grew in numbers around the world. His solution was to exile John to the island of Patmos in the Aegean Sea to remove him from the spotlight and out of contact with the world.

Domitian's plan was a good one, but God had a plan as well for it was on this island that John received his vision from God that ultimately became the book of Revelation.

John the Retiree

History tells us that John outlived all the rest of the disciples. He was successful in avoiding death by persecution, likely dying in Ephesus between 95-100 AD. If he was around twenty years old when he was called by Jesus in the year 30 AD, that would put John around 90 years old when he passed away.

Imagine his life. He started out a lowly fisherman with no thought of doing anything but living in the same area and doing the same job for the rest of his days. His life took a dramatic turn when he walked away from his fishing nets after accepting Jesus's invitation to follow and for the next three years he was in constant, close contact with the man that upended the religious status quo. Constantly threatened by those in power, John stayed with Jesus until his death and resurrection. Then, rather than returning home to resume his career as a fisherman, he continued proclaiming this new message to anyone, everywhere around the world. Even when persecution intensified, he continued to press on because his cause was literally life and death for people, eternally. He strengthened an unknown number of churches and was key to the Christian message spreading around the world. Even being exiled to an island prison could not stop this man.

He was, in one word, devoted.

Chapter 1: An Introduction to Revelation

There is a common writing style among most of the books of the New Testament, particularly those that were originally letters written to the early churches. The first section of these letters introduce the author; the intended audience; a few words of greeting; and a section that sets the theme for the remainder of the letter.

Chapters 2-3: The Seven Churches

The seven churches that the book was written to were established in towns in what was known as "Asia Minor" and is today the country of Turkey. The churches were referred to by the name of the town in which they were located. Contrary to our modern-day understanding of churches, these churches probably lacked a dedicated building, and instead, were located in someone's house. The seven towns were Ephesus, Smyrna, Pergamum, Thyatira, Sardis, Philadelphia and Laodicea.

These churches were on the same Roman mail/trade route, which likely meant that there was an established road between the cities.

Traveling therefore, would have been easier than travel between other towns, and the time required to travel between the towns was diminished as well.

After presenting Jesus as a powerful conqueror in Chapter One, why doesn't the book jump right into the things most people seem to want to know about – the end times? First, a foundation needed to be laid regarding the state of the church in John's time. The next part develops a solid foundation for the message of encouragement and hope.

What did we find in Chapter One? We found a picture of a powerful and conquering Jesus standing in the midst of His Church. It is through His church that He knows the battle against satan will take place. It is no fluke or just filler material that Revelation starts out addressing His church. The battle satan is waging is not one that is just fought in the heavenly realms, it is fought in the trenches on earth. Satan is battling Christians and the church. Jesus knows that if His church is to be strong and victorious over satan, it needs to realistically face the challenges that lie before it. That message was concrete and clear to the churches in the first century and it is still sound and clear in the 21st century.

As we've discussed, each city where a particular church was located had its own unique characteristics, some of which offered challenges and temptations to those who were believers. Ephesus was probably the largest and leading church in the region.

There could be a reason that seven churches were selected. In prophetic writings like Revelation, as well as Old Testament writings like Daniel and Ezekiel, numbers were also symbolic of certain things. The number 7 was used to symbolize completeness or sometimes perfection. The seven churches were not perfect churches but as a whole they presented a complete picture of the challenges that Christians were facing in the days of John and that Christians are facing today. At the end of each letter to the church it ends with a admonition to all the churches – "Hear what the Spirit says". Each one of the messages was relevant to all Christians then and now.

So, as we looked at each of these churches we learned some interesting history and saw how Jesus's words directly connect to the life they lived and the challenges they faced.

Chapters 4-5: The Throne Room of God

John's letters to the seven churches in Asia were what we would describe as "wake-up calls". The churches had their problems. They had their distractions. But for them, worship was not simply a hassle to get ready for, it was potentially dangerous. They weren't going to worship with elevated blood pressure because of the stress of getting ready for church; they walked in wondering how to protect themselves and their children from persecution from the Roman government and the local authorities.

Is it any wonder that right after John addresses the seven churches that the angel then focuses on worship? They needed to be reminded of what it was all about.

Today we are living in the middle of what some Bible scholars have called the "already and not yet". We have already seen the work of God and His blessings but we have not yet experienced everything that He promises.

What are we to be doing while waiting? John said to the church at Ephesus, "Be thou faithful unto death and I will give thee the crown of life." (Rev 2:10, KJV). Revelation moves from a message to the churches into the sanctuary of worship. In Revelation 4 - 5 we find what is called the throne room scene and we need to discover what can be called "Whole-hearted" worship.

Chapters 6-16: Judgment

We know what you're thinking: "FINALLY! The good stuff!". And yes, this section, this long section, is full of symbolic language, war, destruction, judgment, and tons of other scenes that have been debated for centuries. The following are found within this section:

- The Seven Seals (Chapters 6-7)
- The Seven Trumpets (Chapters 8-11)
- The Woman, the Dragon, the Beasts, the Lamb, the 144,000, and the harvest of the Earth (Chapters 12-14)
- The Seven Bowls (Chapters 15-16)

You'll note a lot of usage of the number seven throughout the book of Revelation. This likely speaks to symbolism. Will there actually be seven trumpets blown? We won't know until it happens, but a more likely definition is that it speaks to the entirety of the event. As was stated previously, for the people of the Old Testament and New Testament, the number seven symbolized completeness. This speaks to our time as well: How many days are in a week? When we think about a complete week, we think in terms of seven days.

Chapters 17-19: Fall of Babylon

At this point in John's vision, the wrath of God is nearly finished but there is one foe left to vanquish. The vision is largely symbolic, but is generally understood to be the evil of this world rather than a physical city of Babylon. Chapter 17 describes the evil while chapter 18 describes the downfall of evil. Chapter 19 is the embodiment of the message of the book of Revelation as there is much rejoicing about the destruction of evil.

One thing in particular for further learning is the somewhat conflicting accounts of the "great multitude in heaven shouting: 'Hallelujah! Salvation and glory and power belong to our God, for true and just are his judgments. He has condemned the great prostitute who corrupted the earth by her adulteries. He has avenged on her the blood of his servants.' And again they shouted: 'Hallelujah! The smoke from her goes up for ever and ever.'" (Revelation 17:1-3, NIV). But considering the persecution that these faithful believers experienced from evil personified on Earth, perhaps it's not too difficult to understand. The rejoicing over evil's fall is probably also tied in to the next section, the judgment of satan, because it symbolizes the beginning of the "We Win" section.

Chapters 19-22: We Win!

If you're one of those who want to know the ending of a book or movie before you watch it, then go read chapters 19, 20, 21, and 22 of the book of Revelation. The image here is tremendous: God's victory over evil and satan have ushered a new heaven and a new earth into existence.

Consider the following:

- "He will wipe every tear from their eyes. There will be no more death or mourning or crying or pain, for the old order of things has passed away" (Revelation 21:4, NIV)
- "The city does not need the sun or the moon to shine on it, for the glory of God gives it light, and the Lamb is its lamp. The nations will walk by its light, and the kings of the earth will bring their splendor into it." (Revelation 21:23-24, NIV)
- "And they will reign for ever and ever." (Revelation 22:5, NIV)

Sign us up!

_____

Dig Deeper: Questions to Consider

While we will cover the entire book of Revelation eventually, with this first book, we felt it important to provide a high level description of the major sections in Revelation. We hope that this chapter has been informative.

Let's discuss what you have learned, either from our writing or your own research. Remember: We highly recommend reading this book with a group of people so that opinions can be jointly developed from (positive) group-think.

1. Which condition of the seven churches most clearly resembles your home church? No cheating by saying that your church is perfect and isn't similar to any of the churches in Asia. These exercises are called "forced choices" and while not always comfortable, they do generate quite a bit of thought. Is your church an Ephesus? Philadelphia?

2. This is a risky question, but we are going to ask it anyway. What is the closest you have been to the worship as described in the throne room of God sections? The closest for Roger was a tie between a Hillsong United concert in Minneapolis or any of the multiple David Crowder concerts he has attended. How about you? Why did you select that as your answer? What was different about that event?

3. What other books about Revelation have you read? Which have been more on point than others? Do you read for accuracy (such as wanting to know the exact definition of the Four Horsemen) or do you read for general understanding?

4. Is there anything you consider to be missing from the book of Revelation? The plot line is solid, at least compared to a Hollywood blockbuster. You have the protagonists, the antagonists, conflict, war, and a victory party like no other. Besides the obvious question of what does all the symbolism mean, what questions do you have regarding the book that aren't answered?

PART EIGHT

BIBLIOGRAPHY & NOTES

Bibliography / Notes / Resources

General Bibliography / Notes / Resources:
- Unless otherwise noted, all Scripture quotations are from THE HOLY BIBLE, NEW INTERNATIONAL VERSION®, NIV® Copyright © 1973, 1978, 1984, 2011 by Biblica, Inc.® Used by permission. All rights reserved worldwide.
- Bruce's writings are assumed to be attributed solely to his creation except in circumstances where he provides annotation for the author of the work.

"Preface" Bibliography / Notes
- Webster's definitions of the words "chaos" and "thriving" were pulled from the website: https://www.merriam-webster.com/.

"How Then to Thrive" Bibliography / Notes
- This section was modified from the "Thriving Amidst Adversity" series by Roger VanderKolk. Most of the text was written by Bruce VanderKolk, Roger's father. These books are available on-line at www.blauwshackmedia.com.
- Although we both have a fairly positive outlook on life, society is increasingly drifting away from Biblical principles and we believe life for believers is going to be more challenging as the Earth continues to rotate around the Sun. Therefore, we felt Bruce's writings on how to thrive in the face of adversity were relevant for this book's audience.

"Revelation's Relevance" Bibliography / Notes
- N/A

"Deep Dive into Revelation" Bibliography / Notes

- "What to Study" - As mentioned in the text, there are a limitless amount of resources on the book of Revelation. A few of these resources don't start and end with Scripture however, and are generally not worth the paper upon which they are printed. If you are looking for additional resources, consult your pastor. If you don't have a pastor, then start your on-line search with a reputable, Biblically-based organization. Or, if you'd like, don't hesitate to drop either of us a note on the Contact section of our website.

- The following is a list of material that we have found helpful, but is by no means an exhaustive list:

  - Study Bibles - We tend to use the NIV version as our primary translation, but any translation would be appropriate. The value of these Bibles is that they provide context to the books, chapters, verses, and words.

  - "The MacArthur New Testament Commentary by John MacArthur" - There are two volumes as the material for the book of Revelation is tremendous.

  - "Revelation" - By John MacArthur - This particular volume is a part of Mr. MacArthur's commentary on every book of the Bible. These offer a condensed commentary but are still very helpful in understanding the text. We also found value with the commentary on the book of Genesis because of the overlay between the original Garden of Eden and the end of the story as outlined in the book of Revelation.

  - "The Book of Revelation for Dummies" by Larry Helyer, PHD and Richard Wagner. What can we say; this book appears to be written specifically for us. This gives a good overview in an easy-to-read and well-put-together format.

  - A good, quality on-line search tool. There seem to be an infinite amount of people that have something to say about Revelation. Enter your specific question into the search engine and read those who have Biblically-sound theories and ideas.

"Introduction (Revelation 1)" Bibliography / Notes
- "Chain of Custody" definition taken from National Institute of Standards and Technology (NIST) website.
- Map of the area detailing locations of Patmos and the seven churches was created by hand by Jeff Chitwood.
- "The Author" Section - Both of the Greek definitions used in this section were gleaned from Vine's Expository Dictionary of Biblical Words, Copyright @ 1985, Thomas Nelson Publishers.
- The definition of words are pulled from Webster's on-line dictionary (www.merriam-webster.com).
- "Where Art Thou" - The information from this chapter is commonly held knowledge. Specific figures, such as the dimension of Patmos and the distance from the mainland, were pulled from multiple sources and researched to ensure commonality.

"Ephesus" Bibliography / Notes
- N/A

"Smyrna" Bibliography / Notes
- The Open Doors report mentioned in the "Persecution Today" section was found at the following website on August 20, 2023: https://www.opendoors.org/en-US/theadvocacyreport/. We encourage you to download the report and add the global persecuted church to your prayer list.
- Points to Ponder with Jeff" - The book that is referenced is "Revelation: A Manual of Spiritual Warfare" written by Max Doner. This book is well-written and a must read if you want to dive deeper into the spiritual battle at play in Revelation and our world today.

"Pergamum" Bibliography / Notes
- N/A

"Thyatira" Bibliography / Notes / Resources:
- N/A

"Sardis" Bibliography / Notes / Resources:
- N/A

"Philadelphia" Bibliography / Notes / Resources:
- N/A

Laodicea" Bibliography / Notes / Resources:
- N/A

"Afterword" Bibliography / Notes:
- N/A

"Bonus Sections" Bibliography / Notes:
- "The Author" - Much of the background into John's story after the ascension of Jesus into heaven is based on tradition and is such common knowledge.
- General Breakdown of Revelation - We intentionally glossed over chapters 6-16 in this book to cover it in a future book. If you're enjoying this book, you will love that one so make sure that you are one of the first to hear about the launch by signing up for our newsletter.

www.ingramcontent.com/pod-product-compliance
Lightning Source LLC
Chambersburg PA
CBHW051516120626
46551CB00012B/952